# HOW TO MAKE TEAMWORK WORK

## Targeting Team Members' Roles to Get The Best Results

**Five 20-Minute Self-Study Sessions That Build the Skills You Need to Succeed**

### FEATURING

Built-In Learning Reinforcement Tools

Case Studies

Personal Productivity Exercises

Customized Action Plan

Individualized Skill Assessments

COVER ILLUSTRATION: RANDALL ENOS

DARTNELL is a publisher serving the world of business with books, manuals, newsletters and bulletins, and training materials for executives, managers, supervisors, salespeople, financial officials, personnel executives, and office employees. Dartnell also produces management and sales training videos and audio cassettes, publishes many useful business forms, and many of its materials and films are available in languages other than English. Dartnell, established in 1917, serves the world's business community. For details, catalogs, and product information write:

THE DARTNELL CORPORATION
4660 N. Ravenswood Avenue
Chicago, IL 60640-4595, U.S.A.
Or phone (800) 621-5463 in U.S. and Canada

This publication is designed to provide accurate and authoritative information in regard to the subject matter covered. It is sold with the understanding that the publisher is not engaged in rendering legal, accounting, or other professional service. If legal advice or other expert assistance is required, the services of a competent professional person should be sought.

*— From a Declaration of Principles jointly adopted by a Committee of the American Bar Association and a Committee of Publishers.*

ISBN #0-85013-290-8
Library of Congress #97-066737

Printed in the United States of America by the
Dartnell Press, Chicago, IL 60640-4595

# INTRODUCTION

**S**ince the early 1980s, U.S. businesses have been learning a simple lesson: Teamwork works. More than 91 percent of *Fortune* 1,000 companies use some form of work team — and they get great results.

Scores of service companies, including Federal Express and IDS, have boosted productivity by as much as 40 percent since adopting work teams. According to Procter & Gamble managers, P&G plans with work teams are 30 percent to 40 percent more productive than their traditional counterparts.

Smaller companies report equally positive results. Johnsonville Foods, a sausage manufacturer in Sheboygan, Wisconsin, claims productivity improved 50 percent since implementing teams.

So chances are today you are a member of a team. It may be a permanent, high-powered, self-managed work team that has day-to-day responsibility for managing itself and the work its members do. Or it may be a special-purpose team that meets only long enough to tackle a particular problem, such as introducing new information technology into your company or identifying changes in work flow that can lower costs and improve the finished product.

No matter which type of team you belong to, this workbook was created with you in mind. *How to Make Teamwork Work* gives you a chance to test your knowledge of the basics of teamwork — and to master skills that will make you a more valuable member of your team. You'll discover basic procedures and skills needed to launch your team and refine the skills you need to be a top-notch team player.

Teamwork skills are invaluable. A recent survey of 125 companies in 34 industries revealed that employers rate *team player* as the number one workplace value. Conducted by international outplacement firm Challenger, Gray & Christmas, Inc., the study discovered that nearly 40 percent of the bosses and managers surveyed ranked *team player* as top among seven desirable work traits. Moreover, 80 percent chose it as either first, second, or third.

But teamwork is still a stretch for many people — especially those of us raised in a culture that values individual over collective accomplishment. When you form or join a team, you are venturing into uncharted territory. As one consultant points out, there are no crumbs in the forest to guide you. Whether you feel frightened, liberated, confused, or fascinated by the team process, *How to Make Teamwork Work* will help you discover its power to transform your company and your career.

# CONTENTS

## 5    WORKING WITH OTHERS OUTSIDE YOUR TEAM    65

## CONCLUSION: YOUR ACTION PLAN    83

# 1

# Off To a Great Start

In this session you will accomplish the following:

- **Grasp the importance of your team's mission and purpose**

- **Identify stakeholders who have an interest in your team's output**

- **Draft a mission statement to guide your work**

- **Set realistic and measurable goals**

- **Learn how to develop a work plan to help keep projects on track**

- **Understand the importance of accountability and empowerment**

- **Find out how to make your first meeting a success**

- **Understand the phases of a team's life.**

## UNDERSTANDING YOUR PURPOSE

"Why are we here?" is one of the most famous existential questions of all time. It is also the most pertinent question a team can answer.

To get off to a good start, newly formed teams simply must spell out their purpose and the short-term goals needed to achieve that purpose. Without a purpose or goals, your team will lack focus and may drift aimlessly.

Your team's purpose is the overall reason the team exists. Goals are the short-term actions the team must carry out to fulfill its purpose. "To improve customer service" might be your team's purpose; "answer every call within three rings" might be one of several goals that help you carry out your purpose.

Purpose can be expressed in a short statement called a mission statement. Here is how three different teams used mission statements to express their purpose:

- "To provide superior service to all personnel through the administration of salary, benefits, and educational and career enhancement programs, and to provide equitable resolutions to job-related problems" (a human resources work team).

- "To achieve a 99 percent on-time delivery rate for all domestic shipments (a team assigned to improve shipping and logistics).

- "To make our credit-approval process more customer-friendly and more accurate" (credit-processing department work team).

Besides stating your purpose, your mission statement reflects the expectations of your team's stakeholders. A stakeholder is anyone who has a vested interest in your team's product, processes, or results. Stakeholders include managers and customers, as well as teammates, support organizations, and special-interest groups. You, too, are a stakeholder.

Before you identify your mission, take a moment to identify your team's stakeholders. Who has a vested interest in your team's work? Who will benefit from the results?

| Stakeholder | How does stakeholder benefit? |
|---|---|
| MAGISTRATE AGENTS | |
| AUDITORS | |
| TP's | |
| MANAGER | |
| CREDITORS | |
| THE TEAM | |

## CUSTOMERS AND YOUR PURPOSE

Who are your customers, and what do they want from you?

These are important questions to answer before you determine your purpose or begin the process of setting goals. Your purpose should reflect the needs of your customers — and your goals should outline specific ways to meet those needs.

To make sure your purpose and goals are aligned with customer needs, consult with your customers first. Ask them how your team can better meet their needs. Use surveys, complaint forms, follow-up calls, and suggestion programs to discover and monitor the needs of both internal *and* external customers. Get to know their expectations, values, and priorities. Then listen. Open your ears, and you will gather important information that will clarify your goals. Use this knowledge to guide the decisions your team makes about the projects it will tackle and the outcomes it desires.

Who are your external customers?

_____

_____

_____

_____

What internal departments or individuals benefit from and rely on your team's services?

_____

_____

_____

_____

What steps can you take to discover more about their expectations, values, and needs?

_____

_____

_____

_____

# WRITING YOUR MISSION STATEMENT

Doesn't seem like it would take long to write a sentence or two, does it? But mission statements are deceptively simple. It takes time to express your purpose and distill it into a short, memorable statement. Don't rush the process. Take time to clarify your mission. A team united by a single purpose and mission will find it easier to set goals, tackle problems, and produce results.

What is your team's mission? Write down your thoughts about your mission, and ask teammates to do the same. Take steps to formulate a mission statement that specifies where you are going and why. When everyone agrees on the same objective, your purpose will be clear — and your mission statement will be ready to commit to paper.

_____

_____

_____

_____

Once your purpose is clear and your mission statement has been drafted, your team will be ready to move on to its next priority: setting goals. Goals are the short-term actions that the team must carry out to fulfill its overall purpose. If your team's purpose is to save money, your goals will outline specific ways to save. If your assignment is to develop a new product, your goals will break the new-product-development process into achievable steps.

## W H A T ' S   Y O U R   G O A L   I . Q . ?

The "A" team at First National Bank has been asked to implement a new credit-processing work flow that will save money and turn loans around quicker. Which of the following goals best states their assignment?

**A. Find ways to shave time and money from current loan-approval procedures.**

**B. Clear up the loan backlog by delegating credit approval decisions to a "hit team" of three decision makers.**

**C. Process all loans in two working days by installing an "expert" computer program that makes simple credit-approval decisions and cross-training team members to handle 90 percent of credit-approval functions.**

**Answer:** *Goal C best meets the criteria for an effective goal.*

To be effective, goals need to possess these characteristics:

• **They are specific.** A goal can be useful only if it specifically states what is to be done and when.

• **They are measurable.** Goals are a yardstick that lets you measure your team's progress. That can be done only if goals allow progress to be measured in a specific way.

• **They are results-centered.** In determining goals, concentrate on the results, not on the activities needed to accomplish them.

• **They are realistic.** In its early stages, a team can make the mistake of being too optimistic about how soon results may be attainable. In the end that will hurt a project because deadlines will be missed, work will fall behind, and enthusiasm will lag. Strive to set realistic goals that are within the capabilities of your team.

• **They are challenging.** While your goals should be realistic, they should also be slightly difficult to reach. Aim high to motivate your team to achieve your goals.

Only when your goals are set can your team move on to a plan of action. Goals in hand, you will have a road map that will lead you from one step to the next.

Remember, your purpose, as expressed in your mission statement, is your target. It indicates where you want to be at a certain time. Goals represent incremental, short-term steps toward realizing your vision. Express them in very tangible terms. Instead of saying "improve customer service," say "achieve a 95 percent on-time delivery rate."

Try your hand at goal writing by changing the following vague goals into specific, measurable goals that a team can act on.

Generate new leads. _____

_____

Cut procurement costs in half. _____

_____

Improve employee health. _____

_____

Save department money. _____

_____

Lower the company accident rate. _____

_____

Now, take a look at your team's mission statement. Develop a list of short-term goals that will help you reach your purpose and mission.

1. _____

2. _____

3. _____

4. _____

5. _____

6. _____

DEVELOPING YOUR TEAM'S WORK PLAN

Specific, measurable goals don't just help you accomplish your mission. They also organize your team's efforts by setting out the tasks that will be required to meet them.

From its goal list, your team should generate a list of projects and tasks and assign them to specific team members. Follow the guidelines in Session 2 to make sure that everyone on your team understands his or her role and responsibilities in accomplishing the work of the team.

Keep in mind that not all members necessarily have to have the same goals to achieve your team's mission. While one member concerns himself with streamlining and improving parts delivery, another may focus on improving parts. Members should prepare brief statements outlining their primary goals, ensuring that each member's goal complements the mission. Everyone on the team shouldn't be playing first base, but everyone should be in the same ballpark.

Stop and think for a moment about your team's work. Reflect on your mission and your short-term goals. What actions need to be taken to make those goals happen?

_____

_____

_____

_____

_____

Which of these actions is your responsibility?

_____

_____

_____

_____

What personal goals can you set to achieve the actions you are responsible for?

_____

_____

_____

_____

_____

# FROM TEAM MISSION TO ACCOMPLISHED PROJECT

These 10 steps can help your team keep its projects on track.

**1. Set a clear goal for your project.** Make it specific.

**2. Determine the project objectives.** Each member should have specific short-term objectives that all point to the overall project goal.

**3. Establish checkpoints.** Don't let the project wander off in different directions. Checkpoints help to keep the project on track.

**4. Make a chart of your project schedule.** List activities and when they need to be carried out. This visual aid keeps the project in focus.

**5. Specify completion requirements for projects and assignments.**

**6. Cheer each other.** Through mutual support, help each other through the highs and lows.

**7. Keep everyone informed.** Post deadlines and meeting times.

**8. Make the most of conflicts.** Build from common ground and focus on issues, not personalities — the *what* of a problem, not the *who*.

**9. Empower yourself.** Each person has expertise. Use it!

**10. Take risks and be creative.** Project teams should look for ways to make breakthroughs. Look for the new and untried approach.

# ACCOUNTABILITY

An important part of your work plan is accountability. Your team needs to agree on how to reach its goals and how each team member will be responsible to the other members and to their organization.

Your level of accountability may vary depending on whether you belong to a self-directed work group or a special project team. If you are a member of a work group, then you and your co-workers are individually accountable for your work. On a special project team, members share accountability.

The elements of accountability include:

- **The values and beliefs by which the team lives.** Everyone on your team has expectations. Those expectations must create a set of values that drives your team to achieve its mission. Everyone must endorse these values and communicate them frequently.

- **Operating agreements or ground rules that define work behavior.**

- **Project planning to guarantee the completion of all work on time.**

- **Implementation planning to ensure that the team's work will be acceptable.**

Your team should decide what, if any, corrective actions it will take if a member does not live up to this individual accountability.

How are you accountable to your team?

_____

_____

_____

How is your team accountable to its supervisors?

_____

_____

_____

How is your team accountable to its customers?

_____

_____

_____

What can you do to increase your team members' accountability to one another?

_____

_____

_____

What are the consequences for compromising accountability?

_____

_____

_____

| Successful Teams ... | Unsuccessful Teams ... |
|---|---|
| set goals and objectives | have no goals and no direction |
| ensure that each member has clearly defined roles and responsibilities | lack clear roles and responsibilities; duties are poorly defined |
| meet regularly | do not meet regularly |
| have a purpose to meetings | have undisciplined meetings that waste team members' time |
| make decisions by consensus | react to crises instead of anticipating them; points are debated but rarely resolved |

## EMPOWERMENT

Before you can tackle projects and solve problems effectively, you need to know how much authority your team has. In order to carry out its decisions and initiatives, a team needs the authority to do so.

If your employer has granted empowerment to your team, success will be determined by how seriously you take your responsibility.

"To feel empowered is to feel a sense of control, a sense that you have the power to affect the work and the organization," observe Edward Betof and Frederic Harwood, co-authors of *Just Promoted!* (McGraw-Hill). "Rather than feeling helpless, as on the dependent end of a parent-child relationship, employees who are empowered have a sense that they can exert control."

Effective empowerment should engender in you these attitudes:

- A belief that you can improve the organization

- Confidence that good ideas will be implemented

- Confidence that even if your suggestions aren't accepted, they'll be appreciated and acknowledged

- Security that you and your teammates can be trusted with responsibility

- Trust that you're respected for your ideas and judgments.

Empowerment is a gift to you and your teammates. Use it wisely. Recognize that individual involvement by each of you will lead to achievement for everyone. When your team is empowered, and given the authority to implement its own decisions and plans, it can achieve very high results.

Are you empowered? Answer these questions about your team. When you understand the limits of your decision making, you can focus on problems within your sphere of influence — the things you have the power to change.

Is your team responsible for its own goals? _____

_____

Can it develop its own budgets?_____

_____

What kind of approval process must you adhere to if you are proposing a change in work flow?

_____

_____

What have you been empowered to do? _____

_____

Who supports you in your organization?_____

_____

How can you increase that support? _____

_____

## MAKING THAT FIRST MEETING A SUCCESS

Your team's first meeting is crucial. Important business will take place. But it can also be awkward, as members need time to adjust to the situation and feel comfortable. In addition, the whole tone of the group is set in that first hour the team spends together.

If you are asked to help lead the first meeting, include the following activities to get your team off to a good, organized start.

**1. Make introductions.** Have team members introduce themselves, discuss their particular jobs, and explain any expertise they may have. Encourage them to take a few minutes to discuss some personal information, such as their outside interests or hobbies. Such a free exchange helps to put everyone at ease and creates the informal tone that facilitates most team relationships.

**2. Choose a team name.** An enjoyable activity, choosing a name allows team members to relax and share ideas together. Usually, it will break down the tension that exists between people meeting for the first time, and it will often bring out creative and humorous suggestions. In addition, it begins building bonds among team members and formally identifies the team as a group.

While suggestions may be humorous, your team's name is not a joke. It signifies an undying recognition of your achievements and connotes your team's personality and character. Give it some thought. Here are some names that other teams have chosen:

**TIPS:** Technicians in Problem Solving

**PIP:** Purchasing Improvement People

**QUICK:** Quality Unit If the Customer's Key

**RIM:** Recognize, Investigate, Motivate

**3. Elect a team leader and a secretary.** The team votes on a team leader (if one hasn't been appointed in advance). Votes are taken for secretary, who will keep minutes, distribute marketing agendas, and do any other paperwork.

**4. Distribute working kits and supplies.** Some companies do not provide any supplies. Others provide kits with pens or pencils, loose-leaf paper, transparencies, notebooks, folders, and, depending on the project, sometimes even a carrying case.

**5. Review goals and objectives.** Ask a member of management to join the team for this segment to explain what the team should be aiming for, discuss issues of empowerment, and give management support.

## YOUR TEAM'S LIFE CYCLE

Every team passes through predictable cycles of excitement and disappointment, activity and quiet. Get to know these phases so you can recognize and respond to your team's phase.

For example, in the first six months of your team's life, you will want to focus on building skills in group dynamics, interpersonal communications, decision making, and conflict resolution. This is also a good time for skill-based cross-training.

After about 12 months, your team should function competently and confidently on its own. You may begin to select your own members, handle your own budgeting, and deal with customers.

Examine this chart to find where your team is in its life cycle, so you can prepare yourself to experience the different stages. Too many teams give up during the dissatisfaction phase and never accomplish their goals. So hang in there!

| Orientation | Dissatisfaction | Resolution | Production |
|---|---|---|---|
| Excitement is high and the team is ready to charge ahead. | After the initial rush of energy, the team becomes more realistic about the demands, responsibilities, and obligations of teamwork, which can lead to dissatisfaction. | The team has worked through dissatisfaction and now is joined together in a cohesive group. | The team settles in to perform the task it was assigned. Enjoy! |
| **Problem:** Members may be uneasy around each other. May be long moments of silence when everyone is careful not to say anything that might offend. | **Problem:** Conflict may arise. | **Problem:** Disappointment may hit when team members realize that their work will require long hours of research, interviews to back up ideas, and a lot of additional thinking to implement them. | |
| **Suggestion:** Be especially friendly. Wisely used, humor that relates directly to the situation can help. Once the initial tension is broken, team members begin focusing on the task at hand. Conversation begins, questions flow, and the group starts concentrating on the problem it is to solve. | **Suggestion:** Ride out the conflict stage. It is an important part of the team process. Properly handled, conflict can help stimulate the flow of ideas, but you'll want to keep it from causing the group to disintegrate. | **Suggestion:** Be aware that this phase is a normal part of the team process. Prepare yourself and others by reminding the group that disappointment can arise. When it does, take a deep breath — and then dig in and work your way to success and a feeling of accomplishment. | |
| **Your team:** | | | |

Once you identify your team's life cycle phase, reflect on what you can do to tackle the problems or make the most of the opportunities associated with that phase.

What problems are you experiencing?

_____

_____

_____

_____

What can you do to help?

_____

_____

_____

_____

QUICK TIP

## KEEP IT ALL TOGETHER

Arrange to have all team members sit in the same office area, if it's possible. Teams that share the same work space have more open communication, better creativity, and higher morale than those who are physically spread out throughout a workplace.

## EASE INTO YOUR TEAM'S LIFE CYCLE

Follow these guidelines to prevent team problems and to prepare your team for maximum productivity.

- **Set boundaries.** Your team should focus on problems within its sphere of influence — the things it can change. And team members should have a clear understanding of the limits of their decision making.

- **Focus on the job.** Processes are important, but remember that the *job* has to get done. The most critical qualifier of a team's success is its ability to get a high-quality job done.

- **Budget enough time.** Teams need time to get together and talk. Meetings, training, and general briefing may take up to 15 percent of a regular workweek during the first few months of a team's life. Plan accordingly.

- **Go slowly.** Don't try to get everything done within the confines of a team meeting.

- **Avoid big projects at first.** A team needs time to make mistakes and learn from them. But learn from mistakes made on small projects rather than on big ones.

- **Get several things going.** Engage the team in several projects at once. Some won't succeed, but some will. And the team will feel good about the winners.

- **Train, and train some more.** Reach out to get the help you need to develop good baseline skills in communications, such as asking open-ended questions, practicing active listening, and resolving group conflicts.

- **Expect courtesy.** As a member, you should model team etiquette and encourage it among team members.

## E X P E C T   T H I N G S   T O   B E   D I F F E R E N T

When you join a team, you give up some of the comfortable notions that most American workers subscribe to. Be prepared to lose the following:

- **Someone to blame.** The team is responsible for its project and accomplishments. The buck can no longer be passed up or across company structures when problems arise.

- **Status symbols.** As team members, you are working together as equals. There's no room for special treatment.

- **The safety of hierarchical bureaucracy.** The drastic change from a hierarchy to a team where everyone is equal can be uncomfortable for some people. Self-direction brings with it more responsibility and pressure.

What have you given up by joining your team?

_____

_____

_____

What are you gaining as a team member?

_____

_____

_____

Don't shoot first and then draw a bull's-eye around what you've hit! Successful teams know where they are going and have detailed plans for how they will get there. Work with your team so that everyone understands its purpose, goals, and mission.

# 2

# DEFINING ROLES AND RESPONSIBILITIES

In this session you will accomplish the following:

- **Clarify roles and expectations for yourself and other team members**

- **Uncover the expectations of you, your team members, supervisors, and customers**

- **Understand the importance of ground rules in helping a team run smoothly**

- **Learn to delegate individual assignments as a group**

- **Clarify responsibilities in carrying out complex projects**

- **Identify four styles of team members**

- **Learn key team leadership skills**

By definition, *teamwork* means sharing. On a team, responsibilities are less clear-cut than they are in traditional hierarchies. This blurring of the lines is part of the power of teams — but it can also be a liability. Problems emerge when team roles are unclear. Tempers flare when work is duplicated or when important work goes undone.

To succeed your team should take as much time as possible defining the various roles of the team. Before you begin your work, know *who* is to do *what*. When each member understands his or her responsibilities, there will be fewer misunderstandings.

On the other hand, the work you contribute shouldn't be limited by your responsibilities. Every team will face times when all its members have to pitch in to meet an important deadline — like the product team that loaded trucks all night to meet a test-market deadline, even though no one had "truck loader" in his or her job description. In those instances, the last thing you want to say is "It's not my job."

Before you tackle the exercises in this session, take a moment to write down your role on our team as you understand it.

_____

_____

_____

_____

_____

Your answer to this question is probably different from what your team leader or even your fellow teammates think it is. That's because a role is much more than just a list of tasks. It also includes the expectations that you and the other team members have about your job.

In order for your team to achieve its best, you and your team members need to know what others expect of them. When expectations are unclear, conflicts will occur.

**Process role definitions and expectations in the early stages of team development, as well as whenever new members join the team.**

## CLARIFY EXPECTATIONS FIRST

Once your team's goals are set, you need to determine how each team member will contribute to reaching those goals. How will members be responsible to each other and to their organization? These expectations should be clarified *before* your team starts to function. Everyone deserves to know what he or she is expected to do. Find out your roles and responsibilities by seeking answers to these questions in an early meeting:

• What is expected of me?

• How do I fit in?

• What are we supposed to do? What are our priorities?

• What are the consequences for not doing so?

Ask others for their expectations too. Don't guess what teammates, supervisors, or customers want from you regarding quality and output. Ask for the specifics. It will be much easier to meet and surpass expectations if you know what they really are.

What do your teammates expect of you?

_____

_____

_____

_____

What do your supervisors expect of your team?

_____

_____

_____

_____

What do customers want from your team?

_____

_____

_____

_____

What do you expect from your team?

_____

_____

_____

_____

## C L A R I F Y    G R O U N D    R U L E S

An important part of a team's expectations has to do with behavior. Early in the team-forming process, members must determine which behaviors will and won't be tolerated. Without rules of workplace conduct, damaging personality clashes are likely to develop. That's why it is important to set ground rules that regulate how team members interact.

From the outset your team's behavior needs to demonstrate teamwork and genuine concern for others. That's difficult for people who have learned to be competitive both in school and in the job market. Ground rules can ease the transition from individual to team member — and help you get along and be productive.

Ground rules should cover:

- How often your team meets

- The importance of punctuality

- Acceptable team behavior

- Common expectations

- How feedback and criticism will be handled

- How differences will be resolved

- When, where, or whether smoking is permitted

- Whether food can be consumed during meetings

- The consequences for rule infractions.

All of these issues should be discussed openly and a list of rules put together for the team with the understanding that they have been agreed upon and should be followed. But ground rules need not be written in stone. In fact, it will take trial and error to find out which ones work. But once you know which ones do, stick to them!

Setting and communicating clear ground rules will prevent conflict later. If infractions occur, the rules should be reviewed to see if they need adjusting or to assign consequences for those infractions. And don't forget to provide a written set of ground rules to new members when they join. You may take established rules for granted — but unless they are told, new members won't have a clue about how they should behave.

Does your team have ground rules? If not, write down some suggestions here and share them at your next team meeting.

_____

_____

_____

_____

_____

# CLARIFY TEAM ROLES

Teamwork means sharing responsibilities. Sometimes, it also means dividing them up. That's why the most effective teams review and delegate individual assignments as a group.

There are several reasons why this approach is important:

1. Teams can usually make better decisions than individuals since members bring differing perspectives to the table, covering more angles of a topic.

2. Team leaders may not choose the best people when arbitrarily selecting team members for jobs. In addition, members chosen at random may not be motivated to do those jobs.

3. Volunteers are not always qualified for the jobs they apply for. The problem may stem from a lack of understanding about a job's requirements. But before your team selects any individual for any task, first consider the qualities that that person should have. Individuals chosen for any particular assignment should:

   • have related knowledge or experience

   • be highly enthusiastic about the job

   • have a strong incentive to do the job

   • have some say about the jobs to which they are assigned.

As your team begins to match jobs to individuals, it should openly discuss each job and its functions. There are several reasons why this is important. First, all team members should understand the requirements of a job in order to select the best people to fill it. Second, each member should have an opportunity to understand the jobs for which they are applying. Third, group discussions may reveal unique insights that may not occur to every individual member.

It is also important to stress collective effort. Make sure everyone understands that no job is the exclusive responsibility of any one member. While individuals are chosen to handle specific tasks, team members are collectively responsible for all projects.

As each job is defined, have the leader ask for volunteers. Indicate that they will be asked to explain their qualifications. That will discourage many unqualified people from volunteering.

Finally, negotiate responsibilities with job candidates. Team members will be more likely to spot problems or mistakes that others have overlooked. Group reviews can also provide your team with an opportunity to compliment individual members and to encourage them to keep up their good work.

By dividing responsibilities this way, team members will learn how to branch off and work effectively as independent agents of the team. As a result, they will bring more knowledge and expertise back to the group.

## WHAT'S YOUR FOG LEVEL?

Role clarification is especially important when there is ambiguity about individual responsibilities. It is also essential when a new team is being organized or when a new teammate joins an existing work unit. How clear are roles on your team?

|  | Yes | No |
|---|---|---|
| 1. My teammates understand their duties. | ❏ | ❏ |
| 2. We pursue clearly defined missions. | ❏ | ❏ |
| 3. Tasks are sometimes done twice because more than one team member feels responsible for the task. | ❏ | ❏ |
| 4. Work is sometimes overlooked because no one knows who is responsible. | ❏ | ❏ |
| 5. Work has to be done over because important steps have been omitted. | ❏ | ❏ |
| 6. Arguments frequently erupt over how and when certain jobs should be done. | ❏ | ❏ |

If you answered **YES** to numbers 1 and 2, and **NO** to everything else, your team's roles are crystal clear. But if you answered **NO** to 1 and 2, and **YES** to 3, 4, 5, or 6, your team should take time out of its duties to clarify the roles and responsibilities of its members.

Use this four-part formula to help your members clarify their roles.

**1. Set high-quality work standards.** There's less role confusion when teams have set a standard by which the quality of all work is measured. Under quality guidelines, misinterpretations will quickly become apparent and just as quickly be resolved.

**2. Be willing to work outside your defined role.** The mentality of "that's not my job" has no place in a team. Just as you would expect your peers to help you if you needed it — even if their roles didn't call for it — they should be able to expect the same from you.

**3. Distribute assignments evenly.** Part of your role within your team is to carry your part of the load. When roles are created around equally shared work, nothing will fall between the cracks. Rather than distributing work according to the number of tasks, which can be deceptive, do so according to the hours of work each task will take. The result will be a load that is more fairly shared.

**4. Hold regular meetings to openly discuss team roles.** Your team roles should be flexible enough to accommodate for special projects as well as the inevitable change that takes place within your organization. Therefore, regular meetings are a necessity to ensure that the team-role structure always supports the organization's needs.

## R O L E S   A N D   T U R F

When roles on a team overlap, you may find yourself competing for territory. Or, if you were formerly a supervisor or a manager, you may find it hard to share responsibilities that were formerly yours alone — with people who previously reported to you!

Misunderstandings about "turf" are natural in a team environment. A team is made up of highly complex job relationships. People must simultaneously fit in as team players, yet hang on to their piece of turf. Even though they work hard to be team players, they sometimes feel lost in the shuffle.

Clarifying roles can prevent misunderstandings over turf. But if conflict arises, take a moment to reflect on your situation before you decide what to do. Select your confrontations with care. Before you go to the mat with a teammate over turf, ask yourself whether his or her behavior is a pattern that ultimately will impede your long-term agenda. If it is, and it's a battle that is worth the effort, it's smart to speak up about the problem before it escalates further.

When you seek clarification, speak and act professionally. Let your teammate know that your intention isn't to fight him or her, but that you want to more clearly understand your role and his or her role so that your jobs don't overlap — and so that each of you gets proper credit for ideas and innovations.

What "turf" misunderstanding have you been uncomfortable about?

_____

_____

_____

What can you do to clarify each other's roles and resolve the conflict?

_____

_____

_____

## CREATE A JOB JAR

Set up a team "job jar." Create a job jar for your team, like many people have for home-repair tasks. Fill it with projects to be tackled and team problems that need fixing. Address three jobs a month.

## CLARIFYING PROJECT RESPONSIBILITIES

Does your team go "gangbusters" when it is solving problems but fall flat when it needs to implement solutions? Lawrence G. Hrebiniak, Ph.D., a professor at Wharton School, University of Pennsylvania, suggests creating a matrix chart of tasks and individual assignments.

- List each task of the project vertically on the chart; write each team member's name horizontally across the top.

- Ask team members to individually mark the level of responsibility of each person for each task. They should put an *R* under the name of the individual responsible for the task or decision, a *C* if the person must be consulted during the activity, and an *I* for the co-worker(s) who should be informed after a task is completed.

- Compare the individual perceptions of responsibilities to see where there is agreement and disagreement.

- Resolve differences of perceptions.

- Draw up a final matrix to use as a checklist.

## FOUR STYLES OF MEMBERS

Many of the roles played by team members have more to do with basic personality than with responsibility. Most teams are composed of four styles of members, says Glenn M. Parker, author of *Team Players and Teamwork* (Jossey-Bass). You can remember their names by thinking of "the four C's." They are the contributor, the collaborator, the communicator, and the challenger. Find out how each one contributes to the overall health of your team — and which role you play.

### The Contributor

A task-oriented team member who enjoys providing the team with good technical information and data, does his or her homework, pushes the team to set high performance standards, and uses resources wisely. This person freely offers all the relevant knowledge, data, and skills he or she possesses. The contributor makes an excellent team trainer, although he or she can become impatient with teammates who lack his or her fervor. The contributor doesn't let the team down. It's no wonder he or she is often the "old reliable" of a team or work group.

## The Collaborator

The goal-directed collaborator keeps the team on track and focused on the vision, goal, or current task at hand. Whatever must be done, the collaborator is always willing to pitch in. Collaborators realize their contributions are necessary for success but don't require individual recognition. Even if it means changing team goals and plans, collaborators are always open to new ideas and data. And, because they have high levels of self-esteem, collaborators seek out critical feedback. They know that it will help them — and the team.

## The Communicator

The communicator is the glue that keeps the team together. He or she initiates and supports pre- and post-meeting discussions of such nonwork topics as family, vacations, hobbies, and sports. The communicator also uses good-natured jokes, comments, and diplomacy to break tension or smooth over awkward moments and reduce destructive conflict. These positive people see a glass as half-full rather than half-empty. They have a "can-do" attitude. Energy givers rather than energy users, they recognize and praise teammates for their efforts, and provide descriptive, specific, and useful feedback. They also prod others to participate in discussions, deftly defuse conflict, and help the team reach consensus on thorny issues.

## The Challenger

Team challengers swim against the tide. They're open, candid, honest, and above all, deeply concerned about the direction of the team. They very much want the team to succeed, but when necessary they express opposition to the prevailing thinking — always with good intentions. They frequently ask tough "why" and "how" questions about goals and objectives. They are not afraid to disagree with the team leader, and don't hesitate to blow the whistle if a teammate is engaged in unethical activities. But an effective challenger knows when to stop pushing. He or she recognizes when a consensus has emerged and it's time to move on. The challenger who doesn't know when to quit can be obstructive.

## WHO ARE THE FOUR C'S ON YOUR TEAM?

Use the following summary chart to determine whether you are a contributor, collaborator, communicator, or challenger. Then assign each teammate to a category. Do you have someone from every category on your team? If not, can you recruit someone to play the missing role?

| Contributor | Collaborator | Communicator | Challenger |
|---|---|---|---|
| Dependable | Goal-oriented | Unites team | Swims against the tide |
| Enjoys providing information and experience; freely offers relevant knowledge, data, skills | Willing to work outside areas of expertise to benefit the team | A process-oriented worker who listens carefully to others | Is always open, candid, and honest — even when it hurts |
| Makes an excellent team trainer | Derives satisfaction from being part of a successful team | Has an infectious "can-do" attitude; always sees the glass as half-full | Insists on high ethical standards and on meeting team goals |
| Can be impatient with teammates who lack their fervor | Doesn't need individual recognition to be satisfied | Praises efforts of others, gives constructive feedback, and facilitates informal climate | Asks tough *why* and *how* questions; often disagrees, but will support the team consensus |
| You:<br><br>Your teammates: | | | |

## SOME ROLES ARE TRANSIENT

Not every role is a permanent one. Members of any smoothly operating team take on different roles that contribute to the attainment of both short-term and long-term objectives.

**1. Supporting.** If you really want to support another member of your team, you must go beyond simply reinforcing his or her point of view only when you agree with it.

**2. Confronting.** There are times when a person's behavior is detrimental to the success of the team. Another team member may confront the undesirable actions. Confrontation is constructive when it's confined to people's behavior. When it involves another's personality or presumed motives, the outcome is usually one of disruption and resentment.

**3. Gatekeeping.** On almost every team, a few members are assertive while others may be somewhat reticent. As a consequence, certain ideas and opinions are pushed ahead too forcefully. A gatekeeper must emerge. An effective approach: "You folks have expressed yourselves quite clearly. Now, let's hear what some of the others have to say."

**4. Mediating.** A dispute can become so intense that the teammates who are slugging it out no longer listen or respond to each other. At this point an impartial member must step in, not to arbitrate but to illuminate. First, ask permission to interpret each position for each side. The mediating member then asks whether that version reflects the disputant's argument. Such intervention can clarify the real differences and areas of agreement.

**5. Harmonizing.** Some debates get so heavy that the participants don't even realize that they actually agree on some points. The harmonizer analyzes their views to show how close they are to real accord. Next, he or she invites other teammates to join in.

**6. Summarizing.** Occasionally, an entire team can become so immersed in needless conflict that confusion takes over. At this point a clear-minded team member comes forward and sums up the discussion. This gives the group time to breathe, think, and restore confidence in itself and forces the team to look at how it is functioning — something that the group might not have done because it was too involved in details to see the whole picture.

As an individual team member, you may find yourself in a position to play one or more of these various roles. If you do, be sure to step in and do your best. It will help your team move forward.

## L E A D E R S   A N D   F O L L O W E R S

While great emphasis is placed on team leadership, don't forget the value of the roles of those who prefer to follow. Skilled followers are needed as teams flatten organizational structures and banish the old hierarchical structure. While there is room on a team for all kinds of followers, effective followers make the best team players. Which kind are you?

| Sheep | Yes people | Alienated followers | Survivors | Effective followers |
|---|---|---|---|---|
| • passive and uncritical<br><br>• perform assigned work, then await new orders | • lack self-confidence<br><br>• need a leader for direction | • independent thinkers<br><br>• carry out their work roles with disinterest | • play it safe<br><br>• adapt to change but seldom initiate it | • think for themselves<br><br>• take risks<br><br>• go at their tasks with energy<br><br>• can solve problems |

A solid, supportive relationship between team members and their leader is essential to maintaining a productive working team. You and your teammates need to spend time making sure that relationship is developing in a positive, productive manner. Follow these tips to keep your end of the member-leader relationship.

- **Keep your leader informed.** Talk about the good news *and* the bad. When things are going well for your team, provide facts and figures to show that you're on target. When things aren't going so well, suggest how the situation could be improved. Explain potential problems, so your leader can help you prepare solutions. Never let your team leader be last to know.

- **Respect your team leader.** Avoid directly criticizing him or her, especially in front of others. Negative words have a way of ending up on your doorstep.

This doesn't mean you should be a "yes man" or a "yes woman." Being part of a team requires that you feel free to give your opinion on team matters. But, just as you wouldn't want to publicly and bluntly put down a teammate's ideas or thoughts, you should extend the same courtesy to your team leader.

If you want your team leader to give honest consideration to and carefully worded feedback on your own ideas, you should give him or her the same respect.

- **Understand and appreciate your team leader's role.** It's always tough to be in charge in any way. Realize that your team leader has goals to achieve too. He or she also has a supervisor to please, just as you do. Try to show some empathy when your leader encounters problems.

- **Know how your team leader communicates.** Some people are impressed by the written word and, as such, prefer to receive important team communications in writing. Other leaders may be verbal communicators, so they want to hear your ideas straight from your mouth. Still others are action-focused and are more receptive to demonstrations of your ideas.

Know how your team leader processes information so that you can approach him or her at the best vantage point. Your team will benefit from increased support.

- **Keep the "big picture" in mind.** While your team's biggest concern may be getting its project accepted "as is," your team leader has to be concerned with cost issues, organizational goals and plans, and also safety issues. When putting a project or proposal together, address the issues that are important to your team leader. You'll have a greater chance of gaining his or her support.

Your team leader is an integral part of your team. By taking into account his or her personality, problems, and concerns, you will lay the groundwork that will help you create strong bonds to see your team through the uncertain future.

# MAKING THE TRANSITION
# FROM MEMBER TO LEADER

At some point in your life as a team member, you may find yourself in charge of people who are now teammates. Don't expect the road from team member to team leader to be as smooth as glass. You'll need to make adjustments, as will your former teammates. Follow these seven tips for transition:

**1. Recognize that authority affects relationships.** If you try to interact with team members in the exact way that you did before you were a leader, you'll be fighting a losing battle. But the change doesn't have to be a negative one.

**2. Characterize the new relationship.** What kind of team leader do you want to be? How do you want to treat your former teammates, and how do you want to be treated?

**3. Expect resistance, but don't take it personally.** If team members react negatively to the change in your status, give the situation some time. Prove that you're a good leader, and you'll win them over.

**4. Don't assert all your authority at once.** Talk to your co-workers about the change and solicit their ideas.

**5. Learn from experience.** Think about your best boss, and recall what traits made him or her a pleasure to work with.

**6. Talk to other team leaders.** Their styles will vary, so don't try to emulate them all. Pick elements from each that suit you best.

**7. Create a joint vision.** Focus on giving all team members a sense of sharing and building.

The skills that make an effective team leader are not much different than those that make good team members. Team leaders should:

- be quick to develop the trust of their fellow employees

- assume that team members are responsible and competent

- be eager to learn new skills

- have a clear sense of what's right and what's wrong

- give clear directions

- be generous in praising good performance.

Above all, the most important skill you will need as a team leader is the ability to bring out the best in colleagues.

# RECIPE FOR TEAM SUCCESS

In this session you will accomplish the following:

- **Create a climate in which your team can thrive**

- **Discover whether you need to loosen up**

- **Determine your team's personality**

- **Learn to build team trust**

- **Discover ways to increase team cooperation**

- **Build community**

- **Measure and increase your commitment**

- **Build personal and team credibility**

- **Assess your team's spirit.**

Successful teams spend a lot of time on their own "care and feeding." Members constantly work at working together.

As team consultant Suzanne Zoglio, Ph.D., points out, "The trouble with teams is that they are so busy *producing* that they don't take the time they should to look at their own processes, to reflect, and to reevaluate their goals. If a team wants to succeed, it has to stop and reflect, 'What impact is this team having on the organization? What impact is it having on me?'"

In the early stages of your team's life, the focus of your "care and feeding" should be on *building*: building an informal climate in which teamwork can thrive; building trust among team members; building personal credibility; and building the collective spirit and enthusiasm that will help your team achieve its goals.

It will take work. Teamwork is tough for a society grounded in individuality. Our heroes are lone cowboys like John Wayne, not the 12 members of the SPIRIT team who boosted customer satisfaction ratings to 99 percent. Some members accustomed to working alone fail to see the benefits of working as a team and will resist it. They're the ones who say, "I work better alone," and "I have to stand out to succeed."

Be patient and don't judge yourself too harshly. These are new attitudes and challenging tasks. A group of people doesn't become a smoothly functioning team overnight. It takes time for a group of people who are put together to begin working as a team.

What impact is your team having on your organization?

_____

_____

_____

_____

_____

What impact is your team having on you?

_____

_____

_____

_____

_____

What "lone cowboy" attitudes are getting in the way of your team's work?

_____

_____

_____

_____

_____

# COOL, TEMPERATE, TROPICAL—
# WHAT KIND OF CLIMATE DO TEAMS THRIVE IN?

Where do teams thrive? Determine whether the following statements about climate are **TRUE** or **FALSE**.

|  | **TRUE** | **FALSE** |
|---|---|---|
| 1. Teams thrive in an environment in which information is shared. | ❏ | ❏ |
| 2. Teams thrive in an atmosphere in which every member feels included and empowered. | ❏ | ❏ |
| 3. Teams thrive in an environment in which teammates acknowledge and support each other's contributions. | ❏ | ❏ |
| 4. Teams thrive in an environment in which all members feel comfortable saying what they think, whether they are asking for help, sharing new or unpopular ideas, or admitting mistakes. | ❏ | ❏ |
| 5. Teams thrive in an atmosphere in which members handle their own assignments, volunteer to help each other, and solicit feedback from colleagues. | ❏ | ❏ |
| 6. Teams thrive in a climate in which conflict is accepted as normal, but ground rules are followed and disagreements are resolved. | ❏ | ❏ |
| 7. Teams thrive in an atmosphere of trust and respect. | ❏ | ❏ |
| 8. Teams thrive in an environment in which changes in the workplace and the team are discussed openly. | ❏ | ❏ |
| 9. Teams thrive in a climate that values innovation. | ❏ | ❏ |

All of these statements are **TRUE**. Read on to discover how to create this optimum climate in your workplace!

# CREATING YOUR TEAM'S CLIMATE

Your team's "climate" has a lot to do with how well you work together and what results you produce.

One important characteristic of a healthy team climate is informality. When a team is working well, its members like each other and enjoy spending time together. Members talk about team meetings as fun and enjoyable. They come early because they want to chat over a cup of coffee before the agenda begins. And they stay longer when the meeting is over to talk shop or swap stories. The relaxed atmosphere encourages an open exchange of ideas.

There are a number of ways you can help your team create an informal climate.

1. **Help teammates get to know and feel comfortable with each other. Set an example by being open, friendly, and approachable.**

2. **Schedule meetings early in the morning when people have time for coffee and conversation, just before noon so that the group can have lunch together, or at the end of the day when people may want to adjourn to a restaurant.**

3. **Bypass such formal trappings as rigid voting rules and raising hands before speaking.**

4. **Make humor an integral part of your team. Use humor and discussion of nonwork topics as a way to relieve tension and smooth over awkward moments. But avoid humor at the expense of teammates.**

5. **Share the limelight with others after you've played a major role in an important team triumph.**

6. **Work with your leader to see if necessary work resources can be provided without submitting formal requests.**

When your team members enjoy being around each other, your team will be effective. An obvious ease of interaction and communication relaxes team members and enhances their contributions.

# SHOULD YOU "LOOSEN UP"?

Good teams are often made up of people who truly like each other. So, being friendly to teammates in no way diminishes your productivity. In fact, it can improve it by contributing to a trusting team environment. Personal warmth is the key to forging team bonds. Do your teammates interpret your businesslike demeanor as being unfriendly? Take this assessment to find out.

|  | Yes | No |
|---|---|---|
| 1. Do you freely smile and greet teammates when you see them? | ❏ | ❏ |
| 2. Are you willing to poke fun at yourself? | ❏ | ❏ |
| 3. Do you socialize with teammates during lunch or break times? | ❏ | ❏ |
| 4. Do you disclose things about your personal life to show that you're human? | ❏ | ❏ |
| 5. Do you ask teammates about their interests? | ❏ | ❏ |
| 6. Do you sincerely compliment your peers? | ❏ | ❏ |
| 7. Are you aware that work and fun are not mutually exclusive? | ❏ | ❏ |
| 8. Do you realize that cultivating goodwill is critical to doing your job well? | ❏ | ❏ |
| 9. Do you share information with teammates? | ❏ | ❏ |
| 10. Do you share a sense of team play? | ❏ | ❏ |

Total Number of YES Answers _____

A score of eight or more **YES** answers suggests that you connect well with your teammates. A lower score might indicate that your demeanor doesn't foster trust and caring from your colleagues. Don't mistake isolation for professionalism. Don't chill out — warm up!

## WAYS TO WARM UP

**1. Follow the Golden Rule.** Treat your teammates at least as well as you would like to be treated.

**2. Catch people doing the right things.** People like to be winners, and they perform better and more enthusiastically when they feel that they are winning.

**3. Be a better person.** Become more sensitive, open, communicative, honest, and respectful, and you will improve your relationships with teammates.

**4. End acts of disrespect.** Examples include being late for an appointment, not saying "hello" when you pass someone in the hall, and not returning phone calls.

**5. Listen, listen, and listen some more.** Don't think about what you're going to say until you've listened to all that the other person has said. Above all, don't interrupt.

**6. Find out what others want and help them.** Everyone has individual goals. Learn about them and try to help the person achieve them.

**7. Be a role model.** Show that you mean what you say. Failure to back up your words with your actions appears to be hypocritical.

## REMEMBER DALE CARNEGIE

Dale Carnegie, author of the classic *How to Win Friends and Influence People*, developed rules of human interaction that work well today. His philosophy can help anyone who embraces empathy, respect, and an appreciation of others. Follow these tips to warm the interpersonal climate of your team.

• **Become genuinely interested in others.** "For years," writes Carnegie, "you may have built the habit of thinking about what you were going to say next when anyone else was talking." Change that habit, he recommends, and focus on what the other person is saying — to probe for his or her real interests in life.

• **Smile.** Not all smiles are created equal. Carnegie says that an insincere smile fools no one. "We know it's mechanical and we resent it," he writes. "There's nothing like a real heart-warming smile that comes from within and brings a good price in the marketplace."

• **Let others have the floor.** Carnegie tells of the successful Texan who said, "I never learned anything new when I was doing all the talking." This doesn't mean simply listening — it means encouraging the other person to talk by asking questions and offering reassuring responses.

## USE SMALL TALK

Small talk is the short, casual warm-up conversation that precedes more in-depth discussion. It isn't trivial chatter. It's a way to build trust, rapport, and loyalty among colleagues. To converse more successfully, find out about the personal and professional interests of those around you. Remember, people like to talk about themselves! A question about an interest, a recent vacation, or a current event can break the ice and create a friendly atmosphere. As you listen to the reply, remember. Successful small talk also requires that you remember what others have said so you can follow up on the topic in the next conversation. Your co-worker will appreciate your interest and amazing memory. It's highly complimentary to recall what others have told you.

## BUILDING TEAM TRUST

For a team to excel, its members must trust one another. The trust that makes a team strong isn't something that just happens — it has to be built up over time. You can start building it by following these six steps:

**1. Maintain each other's self-esteem.** Encourage your teammates when they are down. Point out how they fit into the big picture.

**2. Support and praise one another.** One of the best ways to encourage peers to rely on you is to ask for help yourself.

**3. Keep sensitive information confidential.** How can teammates trust you if you can't keep a secret?

**4. Stand up for each other.** Let others know that your team stands together in success and failure.

**5. Avoid gossip and unfair criticism.** If you earn a reputation as a gossip, your team will never share anything with you.

**6. Appreciate one another's differences.** Each member makes up a separate and equally important part of the team.

This last step — appreciating each other's differences — is absolutely critical to building team trust. As Helen Keller once observed, "The world is moved not only by the mighty shoves of the heroes, but also by the aggregate of the tiny pushes of each honest worker." In other words, it takes all kinds.

Teams need some members who are strong in technical skills. But they also need self-leaders, people who can do what it takes without being told, and informal leaders who step forward and take charge when it's appropriate. When there's a diverse balance of talent, a team can tap the wide range of ideas and talent present to booster its overall performance.

Each of your teammates is a uniquely gifted *individual*. When personal job skills are integrated into one finely tuned workplace machine, winning teamwork results.

Take a moment to reflect on the gifts of each of your teammates. Don't forget to list yours, too!

**Teammate**_____

**Gifts**_____

_____

**Teammate**_____

**Gifts**_____

_____

**Teammate**_____

**Gifts**_____

_____

**Teammate**_____

**Gifts**_____

_____

**Teammate**_____

**Gifts**_____

_____

**Teammate**_____

**Gifts**_____

_____

**Teammate**_____

**Gifts**_____

_____

**Teammate**_____

**Gifts**_____

_____

**Your gifts**_____

_____

## COOPERATION: THE NAME OF THE GAME

For you and your team to succeed, cooperation among teammates is paramount. And the responsibility to work together effectively rests with everyone on the team.

Follow these helpful techniques to nurture a cooperative team atmosphere:

• **Recognize that nobody is perfect.** Not even you. When Lee fails to thank you for helping with an urgent project, don't take it personally. You might do the very same thing tomorrow when your schedule is busy and you are so preoccupied that you forget to acknowledge Lee's assistance. Actively try to avoid such oversights whenever possible.

• **Consider other viewpoints.** If you, as a co-worker, ask Ruth to help you with some extra work, return the favor. If Ruth becomes frustrated because of her heavy workload, ask her if there is anything you can do to help — or help her find assistance.

• **Admit your mistakes and faults.** A co-worker is more likely to give you a helping hand to correct a mistake if you take responsibility for it rather than blame someone else. You don't want someone to think, "Why should I help? If something goes wrong, I'll probably get blamed!"

• **Listen to what your colleagues say.** Sometimes co-workers just need a supportive ear to listen to their problems. Often just listening to a team member vent feelings can be a big help, even if you don't necessarily commiserate or agree. When listening, don't interrupt; do offer constructive feedback. (Find out how to give it in Session 4.)

## GIVE UP CONTROL TO WIN COOPERATION

We all have the desire to control situations — and other people — now and then. But giving in to that urge for control can be very destructive to the cooperative spirit required for teamwork, especially when conflicts arise. To foster team cooperation:

• **Be open-minded.** Show your willingness to change and see things from other people's points of view, even when you feel strongly about an issue. For the sake of peace, be receptive to considering a third alternative — one that's different from either person's original position.

• **Communicate assertively by saying exactly what you mean and in a way that shows respect for others.** For example, always identify how you feel, whether it is positive or negative: "I'm disappointed," or "I'm really impressed with your idea." Make sure to take responsibility for your feelings by using "I," as in "I'm confused," or "I'm not clear on what you mean." Using "you," as in "you've confused me," will put the other person on the defensive.

• **Clarify feedback you receive.** Sometimes that means exploring vague criticism leveled at you, such as "I just can't work with you." It may take courage on your part, but you need to find out what the real problem is so that you can get beyond it. Ask for specifics: "What is it about me that you can't work with?"

- **Work with rather than against people's differences.** It's amazing how many communication difficulties can be eased by shifting from "He/she is wrong" to "We're different. Now, how can we work productively together, taking differences into account?"

- **Don't try to change others.** So much conflict arises from our efforts to change people when they don't live up to our expectations. In both our personal and professional lives, accepting others as they are is the foundation for a cooperative relationship.

Think of a recent situation in which you and a team member differed. Take a moment to acknowledge the differences between your two positions. Then see if you can find a way to benefit from the difference.

## BUILD RELATIONSHIPS BEFORE SEEKING RESULTS

The pursuit of short-term results may damage long-term relationships — especially if the relationship is sacrificed for the results.

In the long run, an organization's results will usually be maximized if relationships are strong and positive. By maintaining good relationships, team members can help each other time after time.

Teams that strive for quick results often do so without regard for relationships. Members make unreasonable demands, neglect to keep everyone informed of their progress, criticize one another, and undermine organizational objectives.

By contrast, relationship-oriented teams are considerate, understanding, supportive, and proud of their contributions. They realize that strong relationships will spawn future successes.

So don't rush. Take the time to build your team's relationship. It's hard work, but the results will pay off in the end.

## QUICK TIP
## LEARN TO ASK FOR HELP

Don't be afraid to ask for help when you've got more work than you can handle or you could use creative input from your team. Learning how to ask for help is as invaluable a team-building skill as knowing how to offer help.

# HOW'S YOUR COMMITMENT?

Your teammates need to know they can count on you. They are apt to judge your trustworthiness through how well you honor your commitments. This assessment will help you rate yourself.

1. I _____ assign deadlines to any commitments I make.

   A. Always          B. Usually          C. Sometimes          D. Rarely

2. I _____ put commitments in writing to remind myself.

   A. Always          B. Usually          C. Sometimes          D. Rarely

3. When a peer asks me to commit to a project, I feel _____.

   A. Pressured          B. Confused          C. Honored

4. If I doubt I can keep a proposed commitment, I _____.

   A. Don't make it          B. Stall          C. Explain why, if I must

5. Before making a commitment to a teammate, I _____.

   A. Think it through          B. Leave myself an out          C. Get my boss to decide for me

6. I _____ take any commitments I make to others seriously.

   A. Always          B. Usually          C. Sometimes          D. Rarely

7. When I haven't been able to honor a commitment, I _____

   A. Forget about it          B. Always learn something          C. Blame others or outside circumstances

8. The kind of commitments I like to make are _____

   A. The ones that make me look good          B. The ones I feel I can meet          C. None; I try to avoid commitments if possible

9. If I fail to keep a promise, I _____ find a way to make it up.

   A. Always          B. Usually          C. Sometimes          D. Rarely

10. I _____ feel bad when I break a promise to a teammate.

    A. Always          B. Usually          C. Sometimes          D. Rarely

Give yourself two points for the following: **1-A; 2-A; 3-C; 4-A; 5-A; 6-A; 7-B; 8-B; 9-A or B; 10-A.** Give yourself one point for these selected answers: **4-C; 5-B.** A score of 16–20 means that you handle commitments well; 13–15 is good; and 12 is average. Below 12 suggests that your teammates might feel they cannot count on you.

To earn the trust and respect of teammates, supervisors, and customers, you need to be credible. But credibility is fragile and thus easily broken. The following behaviors may compromise your credibility. Are you guilty of any of these credibility killers?

• **Keeping callers on hold.** Credibility is earned with respect. Keeping people on hold doesn't respect their time.

• **Not delivering on promises.** Unless you're sure you can, don't say so. You and your teammates need to follow up on commitments and do what you say you will do.

• **Covering up mistakes.** Most mistakes are honest. Hiding them isn't. Eventually, teammates, supervisors, and customers alike will discover the truth. You will be viewed as much more credible if you "come clean" when you have made a mistake and then do your best to fix it.

• **Not returning calls.** This is a quick way to earn enemies.

• **Breaking confidences.** This is one of the most common ways people lose the respect of others. Eventually, teammates will be reluctant to tell you anything for fear of what you might do with the information. Ultimately, you end up being uninformed.

• **Being disorganized.** This is often perceived as incompetence — even if you know where everything is in your messy office. Poor organizational skills may seem like a minor offense, but if you constantly misplace things, forget appointments, and seem to have trouble managing your work, others will not have much professional respect for you. They may see your chaos as a reflection of your abilities — no matter how competent you are in other aspects.

• **Being late to meetings.** Chronic tardiness usually results in peers viewing you as unreliable. People aren't interested in hearing a wide variety of excuses. They just want you to be where you're supposed to be when you're supposed to be there.

• **Criticizing or embarrassing others.** Public ridicule or making jokes at someone else's expense labels you as mean-spirited and insecure. If you have legitimate feedback to offer someone, do it in private. Anything else is probably better left unsaid.

• **Refusing to consider other viewpoints.** There's no better way to tell teammates that you are inflexible. While there are times we must stick to our guns, often it serves us better to listen to others' perspectives and insights. Imagine the fate of your team if everyone refused to compromise!

• **Failing to help others.** You show that you are not a team player if you don't extend yourself to help co-workers on occasion.

• **Turning in work that is sloppy or late.** Poor execution of specific jobs indicates that you cannot perform your tasks well or that you simply do not care to do the job right. Either way, you look careless.

Don't abuse the trust you've established with peers. Give teammates the same kind of service you would give a supervisor or external customer by returning calls promptly and following up on requests.

List your own credibility challenges. What promises does your team have to deliver in order to build its credibility?

_____

_____

_____

_____

What must team members do to build credibility with one another?

_____

_____

_____

_____

## ESTABLISH A BEHAVIOR CODE THAT TRUSTS AND EMPOWERS

The behavior code discussed in Session 1 clarifies the behaviors that a team will and won't tolerate. It should spell out common expectations, enhance team self-management, and help new members know what is expected. It should also promote the trust, respect, and community that you are seeking to build.

These are the basics of acceptable team behavior you might want to consider including in your team's code of behavior:

- Making "I" statements such as "I feel," "I think," and "I need" (as opposed to such incendiary statements as "you always," and "you never.")

- Listening actively to promote two-way communication

- Respecting others' needs, feelings, and rights through civilized disagreements

- Sharing information and expertise.

By contrast, these are some of the behaviors guaranteed to create team dissension:

- Refusing to set aside personal agendas and work with the rest of the team

- Intimidating teammates by arguing that a situation is an "always" or a "never"

- Displaying a negative attitude toward change, people, and the entire team-building process

- Showing a drive to be an individual star rather than a member of a work unit in which everyone is regarded as equal

- Judging others quickly but being slow to examine one's own behavior.

Team building requires that we change our assumptions about people. Often, the rules of traditional organizations suggest that employees are dishonest and disrespectful, steal, cheat, and satisfy only their own needs.

In a team-building culture, people must be viewed as honest, straightforward, kind, and eager to do the right thing. Incorporate these attitudes into your team's behavior code — as well as its everyday business.

## BUILDING TEAM SPIRIT

Just as a winning team spirit is shared by an entire team, the whole team should share in creating that positive spirit. Try these tips:

- **Find a reason for working together.** Think of how the success of the team project will benefit you personally. What is it about the team goal that will bring you personal satisfaction? Help others discover the answer for themselves.

- **Care about and support your teammates.** Fellow teammates may withdraw and leave participation to others if they don't feel they are an integral part of the process. Encourage participation of others. Listen to their suggestions.

- **Have determination and commitment.** For a team effort to succeed, members need to feel that the group goal is important and that their success together is as important as success separately on any individual project they would be working on.

Don't wait for your leader to take action. Start by taking the first steps yourself!

# TIME OUT FOR A TEAM CHECKUP

Though team members may be working well together, it's still important that your team pause occasionally to evaluate itself as a group. Team members should take this assessment individually, then discuss the answers. Even if all is well, the process of taking the assessment and sharing answers can help build a stronger, more unified team.

|  | Yes | No |
|---|:---:|:---:|
| 1. Has your most recent team project reduced costs, improved a product, or helped improve time management? | ❏ | ❏ |
| 2. Was the project completed on time? | ❏ | ❏ |
| 3. Did your team leader explain problems accurately? | ❏ | ❏ |
| 4. Were all members involved in the problem-solving process? | ❏ | ❏ |
| 5. Was everyone kept abreast of the status of the project? | ❏ | ❏ |
| 6. Did the team seek management approval as needed? | ❏ | ❏ |
| 7. Did the team keep management informed? | ❏ | ❏ |
| 8. Does your team really value the concept of teamwork? | ❏ | ❏ |
| 9. Has communication improved within the team as a result of this project? | ❏ | ❏ |
| 10. Did communication improve between the team and management? | ❏ | ❏ |

Fewer than seven **YES** answers indicates your team may want to spend more time on the team-building techniques in this session.

# 4

# WORKING TOGETHER: THE TEAM PROCESS

## I N T R O D U C T I O N

In this session you will accomplish the following:

- **Learn how to get along with difficult personalities**

- **Evaluate your own style of working**

- **Learn the basics of persuasion**

- **Find out how to give advice without offending**

- **Master the secrets of effective praise and positive reinforcement**

- **Get the most out of giving — and receiving — feedback**

- **Understand the nature of conflict**

- **Use negotiation to resolve conflicts**

## H A V E   Y O U   E V E R   W O N D E R E D   W H Y   M I G R A T I N G   G E E S E   F L Y   I N   F O R M A T I O N ?

When they fly in a *V*, the flap of each goose's wings creates an aerodynamic lift for the bird flying behind. Thus, the flock achieves about 70 percent more flying range than if each goose were to fly alone.

In the same way, co-workers who share a common sense of purpose and direction can get where they want to go faster and easier by providing help to one another — that is, by working as a team and flying in formation.

Successful teams work on the process of being a team. No matter how much talent your team has, it will fail if you don't have a process worked out for building consensus, giving feedback, resolving team conflicts, and handling team crises.

## IS OUR TEAM ON TRACK?

That's a question every team should ask itself periodically. The following 10 questions can serve as a starting point in a team self-evaluation and pinpoint teamwork skills that need improvement.

Try answering the questions yourself first, and consider using this assessment in a meeting. For team members to maintain anonymity, the questions can be answered on paper and typed up together on a master sheet without attribution. Then, at a special team-development meeting, the collected answers can be discussed and corrective action taken. Here are the questions:

|  | YES | NO |
|---|:---:|:---:|
| 1. Do we trust each other? | ❏ | ❏ |
| 2. Are we genuinely interested and concerned for each other? | ❏ | ❏ |
| 3. Do we feel free to communicate openly? | ❏ | ❏ |
| 4. Do we understand our team's goals? | ❏ | ❏ |
| 5. Do we have a real commitment to these goals? | ❏ | ❏ |
| 6. Do we make good use of all our abilities? | ❏ | ❏ |
| 7. Do we handle conflict successfully? | ❏ | ❏ |
| 8. Does everyone participate? | ❏ | ❏ |
| 9. Do we respect our individual differences? | ❏ | ❏ |
| 10. Do we enjoy being members of this team? | ❏ | ❏ |

**Total Number of YES Answers_____**

Fewer than eight **YES** answers may indicate that you need to study carefully the communication and conflict-management concepts and techniques discussed in this session and review important concepts about trust and commitment in Session 3.

## Working with a Team Grouch

Is there a grouch on your team? If so, you know how difficult it can be to work with one.

Still, you do have to work together. Try using these tactics when dealing with an irritating teammate:

- **Don't overreact.** The grouch is looking for someone to irritate.

- **Don't play along.** Stay cool and detached.

- **Defuse the tension.** Use a little humor. Joking in a nonmalicious way can lighten everyone's spirits.

- **Contain the damage.** Team leaders can assign temperamental workers tasks to do on their own so they aren't able to stir up the others.

- **Make expectations clear.** Try to find out what's wrong. The team leader should empathize if a personal problem is causing the behavior, but it should be made clear that such moodiness must be kept out of the work group.

## Handling the Team Complainer

What a headache!

Every team seems to have one or two members who are chronic complainers. Sometimes their gripes are justified, but because they "cry wolf" so often, it's tempting to brush them off.

There is a better way to deal with chronic complainers.

- **Don't dismiss any complaint as being trivial.** Examine it and talk to the griper. Many such people will back off when they're placed under scrutiny, or you'll discover a real problem that needs solving.

- **Ask other team members if they feel that the complaint has any validity.**

- **Act as a sounding board.** Many "gripe specialists" just want to let off steam. As long as they don't bother others, allow them to have their say.

- **If discipline is called for, impose it.** The gripers may claim that you're biased, but you must simply pay no attention.

Another way to handle gripes is to encourage teammates with complaints to work through the problem by filling in these blanks:

1. **My gripe is** _____

_____

_____

2. **My real concern is** _____

_____

_____

3. **What I'm really wishing for is** _____

_____

_____

4. **Therefore, my goal is to** _____

_____

_____

Through the write-it-down therapy, griping teammates can turn negative brooding into positive action.

## Drawing Out the Silent Types

They're members of your team, but because they don't explode with spectacular contributions, their potential is unknown and often remains untapped. They're your "hidden" teammates.

A top-performing team needs the contributions of everyone — the backstage cast of employees as well as the "superstars" who are heard from again and again. Strive to uncover the true capabilities of your silent teammates by using these techniques:

• **Question, dig, and motivate.** Ask your backstage teammates, "What do you really *like* to do and *want* to do in your job? How do you think you can be most important to the team?" Use open-ended questions like these to draw your teammates out into the spotlight.

• **Listen for ideas.** Encourage quiet teammates to contribute to projects and meetings. Don't let the squeakiest wheel get all the grease. Remember that people communicate in their own ways. Your peers may be quietly trying to contribute something. Give them the space to do so.

• **Include everyone in the success.** When you reach a team goal, give credit to everyone. The lack of recognition that most backstagers are used to can cause them to shy further and further away from the spotlight over time. By receiving a taste of stardom, they just might come to like the acknowledgment. Then you won't be able to stop them from contributing!

Remember that a quality team is made up of all kinds of people with all kinds of good ideas to share. Make your team environment one that encourages everyone to shine.

QUICK TIP

GETTING ALONG

If you have to work side by side with a co-worker but you have difficulty getting along, search for a "common ground" such as a mutual interest in sports, a hobby, or a favorite charity. Emphasize your similarities to smooth over the rough edges of your relationship.

CASE #1: NOTHING'S WRONG, RIGHT?

*A member of your work team dislikes you. You hear from others that he has made negative remarks about you. You've asked him if something is wrong but were told "everything is fine." You know better. What should you do?*

_____

_____

_____

_____

Compare your answer to the answer on page 87.

## AM I DIFFICULT TO WORK WITH?

Is it possible that you have a hand in your team's ongoing tensions? Sometimes we are not fully aware of how we appear to others. The following assessment can help you determine whether others perceive you as easy or difficult to work with.

|  | YES | NO |
|---|:---:|:---:|
| 1. Do you count to 10 before reacting when someone makes you angry? | ❑ | ❑ |
| 2. Do you try to smile and be pleasant? | ❑ | ❑ |
| 3. Do you avoid overburdening others with your troubles? | ❑ | ❑ |
| 4. Do you control stress through diet or exercise? | ❑ | ❑ |
| 5. Do you give others the "space" they need when they're having a bad day? | ❑ | ❑ |
| 6. Do you try to monitor your behavior when you're having a bad day? | ❑ | ❑ |
| 7. Is it important to you to work well with others? | ❑ | ❑ |
| 8. Are you someone you like to work with? | ❑ | ❑ |
| 9. Do you greet others by name? | ❑ | ❑ |
| 10. Do you believe the secret to success in teamwork is getting along with others? | ❑ | ❑ |

**Total Number of YES Answers:** _____

Nine or 10 indicates you have a good grip on your gripes. Six to eight suggests you generally are easy to get along with, but teammates may not be sure what to expect on a given day. If you scored lower, you need to try harder to control your emotions. Question 8 is vital: To work well with others, you must first have self-esteem and self-confidence.

## TEAM COMMUNICATION

Like any group of humans, teams communicate about a wide variety of issues. They share jokes and information. They persuade, praise, and sometimes criticize. It's all normal — but there are methods that will facilitate good communication and keep your team working smoothly.

**QUICK TIP**

## SPEAK UP WHEN SOMETHING BUGS YOU

If you're frustrated or angry about a team problem, talk to a peer about your feelings. Sometimes just expressing your concerns can improve your attitude.

## PERSUADING

Within your team you must try to persuade others that your ideas are sound. And when you're dealing with management, skilled persuasion is even more essential.

Follow these tips to persuade effectively.

- Know in advance precisely what you want from the person you wish to persuade. Be specific.

- Determine the amount of time, effort, and money that will be needed to grant your request.

- If what you want is going to be complex and time-consuming, say so at the outset.

- Research the advantages to the other person of cooperating with you.

- Be prepared to respond to any possible objections that may be raised.

- Keep your sales pitch brief. There is a fine line between persuasion and harassment.

- Always assume that your teammate's or supervisor's point of view is valid. You won't win by dismissing questions and objections out of hand.

- Be prepared to negotiate.

Finally, if you strike out, know when to quit gracefully. Many more work days lie ahead.

## SILENCE IS GOLDEN

Well-placed words can have impact, but so can well-timed silences. Silence can make your statements seem well-thought-out, confident, and powerful. You can also avoid conflicts and earn the respect of team members by saying only what's enough.

## WATCH OUT FOR COMMUNICATION KILLERS

When proposing an idea to teammates, beware of "killer phrases" that can stop your project cold. Combat these killers with responses that put your proposal back on track.

- **"Get a committee to look into that."** A committee could sidetrack the development of your idea. Turn it into an advantage by being directly involved with the committee's actions.

- **"Don't rock the boat."** Illustrate the advantages of creating a change. Be specific in identifying the drawbacks of the status quo.

- **"We've tried that before."** It can be difficult to be open to an idea that has flopped in the past. But your advantage is that it happened *in the past*. Make it clear why you think the idea didn't work then and why it will work *now*.

- **"That will never work."** This statement is crushing in any context. Make it clear how it can work and what can be done to ensure the idea's success.

- **"It's not in the budget."** Suggest alternatives to keep the funding low — starting small, for example.

- **"Yes, but ..."** Pay close attention to what follows the "but." Then immediately address that alleged drawback directly and try to change that "but" to a "yes."

- **"The boss will never go for it."** Revise the idea so that your teammates have more confidence in it. Try to look at the situation from your boss's view to find and solve possible problems before you present the idea.

# ADVICE ... WITHOUT OFFENSE

It is not unusual for teammates to find themselves giving work-related advice to co-workers. To find out if you are doing your best to give advice without giving offense, take the following assessment. Simply answer each question **YES** or **NO**.

|  | YES | NO |
|---|---|---|
| 1. Do you avoid taking the lead when a problem arises in your area of expertise? | ❑ | ❑ |
| 2. Do you try the indirect approach at first? | ❑ | ❑ |
| 3. Do you speak quietly so others won't hear you? | ❑ | ❑ |
| 4. Do you first ask the person what he or she wants or needs to know? | ❑ | ❑ |
| 5. Do you refer to your own mistakes in order to put the other person at ease? | ❑ | ❑ |
| 6. Do you "speak with a smile"? | ❑ | ❑ |
| 7. Do you wait for the best time to talk to the other person? | ❑ | ❑ |
| 8. Do you avoid jumping to conclusions about the other person's abilities? | ❑ | ❑ |
| 9. Are you clear and concise in giving your advice? | ❑ | ❑ |
| 10. Do you periodically question the other person to make sure he or she understands you? | ❑ | ❑ |
| 11. Are you diplomatic at all times? | ❑ | ❑ |

**Total Number of YES Answers** _____

Are you a good advisor? Each **YES** answer is worth seven points. A score of 63 or above means that you are a diplomatic co-worker. If you scored 49–62, you are on the right track, but you should review the areas in which you answered **NO**. If you scored below 49 you may need to work on your diplomatic skills before offering advice to a teammate.

# THE CHARACTERISTICS OF POSITIVE REINFORCEMENT

It's far more difficult to keep a team going than to start one. But if you practice peer reinforcement, you're one step closer to ensuring the continued success of your team.

When you catch someone doing something right, phrase your compliment to include these five characteristics.

**1. Specific.** When complimenting a team member on a job well done, be specific. "Hey, you're really great!" will not produce the same efforts as "Your suggestion to change the stations on the production line saved us $300 on the Phillips order. Great thinking!" A pat on the back does alot to bring back behavior we want to see again.

**2. Immediate.** Any time lapse rapidly diminishes the value of positive reinforcement. Tell someone that you appreciate an idea immediately so that the situation and the suggestion are still fresh. Immediacy will also help you be specific about the details of the action.

**3. Achievable.** Peer reinforcement should be delivered based on the individual's ability to achieve, not on a set standard. If a team member does something unusual or exceptional, that's the time to offer praise.

**4. Intangible.** Reinforcement should always be as intangible as possible to avoid conflict. Don't offer something material, such as taking a co-worker out to lunch for helping you at work. Material rewards raise co-workers' expectations. Recognition through verbal praise is the best form of positive reinforcement. The more tangible the reinforcement, the more potential it has to create animosity among peers.

**5. Unpredictable.** Genuine reinforcement is usually spontaneous, since it is delivered only in response to a good idea or action. Scheduled compliments, such as praise at the close of each meeting, seem phony and often have the opposite effect they were intended to produce.

Both positive reinforcement and praise need to ring true to be effective. Doling out compliments won't work well if others don't think you're sincere. When praise backfires, you can breed contempt and strain work relationships. Here are some tips to get your meaning across:

• **Be consistent.** If you don't normally praise people, a compliment out of the blue can breed suspicion. Your co-workers might think you have a hidden agenda and that you're up to no good.

• **Offer compliments voluntarily.** A compliment offered grudgingly or unenthusiastically is worthless. Avoid anything that smacks of tokenism.

• **Avoid the backhand.** Don't dilute praise with veiled criticism as in, "I never expected you could do something that well!"

• **Get personal.** Compliment others privately. Otherwise, you might cause embarrassment or promote jealousy among teammates.

Reflect on your team's recent interactions, and identify teammate contributions you can single out for praise and positive feedback. List four of them.

1. _____

2. _____

3. _____

4. _____

## G I V I N G    F E E D B A C K

Two important parts of being a team player involve letting others know when their actions and ideas are good ones — and telling them tactfully and constructively when they're not.

The key is to direct your comments at the behavior exhibited or concept presented by your teammate rather than at the teammate directly.

Focusing on behavior and actions, rather than traits, makes feedback more acceptable. It leaves the recipient believing that change is possible.

If your feedback is critical, preface it with a positive statement. "I think you're on the right track with that cost-cutting proposal, and it could be even better if …" Notice that the word *and* is used rather than *but* to separate the compliment from the criticism. The word *but* often negates anything said after it.

Base your constructive feedback on:

• something someone does

• something you can see happening

• something that can usually be measured.

Avoid judgmental statements like "You are a sloppy worker." Not only will it make your teammate defensive, it won't help your peer. A measurable behavior on which you could comment might be, "You made 50 percent more errors on this project than the rest of the team."

**Practice making these judgmental statements into constructive feedback.**

You're always late.

_____

_____

That will never work.

_____

_____

I don't think that the new machine is worth the investment. Nobody will use it.

_____

_____

## TRY THE CRITICISM SANDWICH

When you are making a critical observation, include some aspect that you *do* agree with. Better yet, sandwich the critical observation between two slices of praise.

Still, you must be sincere. If, for instance, a co-worker constantly interrupts, tell him, "You're so helpful, but I find myself getting behind in my work because I spend so much time talking to you." Close on a positive note. "Let's get together at our break."

**Build a "sandwich" using these critical statements.**

I think you have been missing too many meetings.

_____

_____

I don't think we can afford to try your idea right now.

_____

_____

It seems like you have been losing important memos lately.

_____

_____

### QUICK TIP
## LEARN FROM MISTAKES

Hear ye! It's important that team members learn from each other's mistakes to reduce the odds of duplicating an error. So when a team member makes a mistake, it's a good idea to let everyone know about it ... but not in a condescending way. Take time out as a team to discuss what caused the mistake and devise methods to keep it from recurring.

"The trouble with most of us is that we would rather be ruined by praise than saved by criticism," said Norman Vincent Peale.

When you are on a team, it will eventually be your turn to be "saved by criticism." It isn't comfortable, but when others extend themselves to be helpful by providing feedback, it's your job to see it as an opportunity to improve. Keep in mind the following guidelines when you hear feedback:

**1. Keep an open mind.** An open mind will help you absorb the information you are hearing. It will also ensure that your teammates are willing to continue to make information available to you.

**2. Listen to understand.** Listen carefully to what is being conveyed so you clearly understand the point. Think about what the person means, and confirm your interpretation by responding, *"So what I hear you saying is …"*

**3. Do not interrupt.** Maximum understanding is achieved through minimal interruptions. If you do interrupt, do so politely and in the interest of clarifying what is being said. Otherwise, make notes for use in seeking clarification later.

**4. Control tendencies to react immediately.** Your best interests generally will not be served by an immediate reaction, either positive or negative, to what is being said. Your initial mission is to seek clear understanding.

**5. Seek further clarification, elaboration, and illustrations.** Feel free to ask your teammate for more information to enhance your understanding. But be careful not to be defensive or argumentative in the process.

**6. Keep reality in perspective.** When someone expresses his or her feelings to you, what is being said is reality to the person saying it. You may feel he or she is being illogical or unreasonable, but remember they are expressing how they feel. That is their reality!

**7. Express your appreciation.** Whether you agree or disagree, appreciate the person's efforts. In essence, you are receiving a gift of information.

**8. Discuss suggestions for improvement.** Your teammate may be a good source of ideas for potential improvement. You may also want to bounce your ideas off of the person — either in your initial conversation or a subsequent meeting.

**9. Change your behavior.** This is more easily said than done. Even minor shifts from old habits may cause anxiety and discomfort.

**10. Seek feedback on progress.** As initial feedback leads to new action steps, continue to seek feedback on performance against new standards.

## W H E N   I S   I T   O K   T O   D I S A G R E E ?

Disagreement within a work team can be healthy, but should you always reveal your conflicting opinion? Take this quiz and find out.

It's OK to express your opinion when …

|  | YES | NO |
|---|---|---|
| 1. You have the facts to back up your opinion. | ❏ | ❏ |
| 2. You are really not sure of yourself. | ❏ | ❏ |
| 3. You don't believe the team has fully examined all possibilities. | ❏ | ❏ |
| 4. You feel strongly about your opinion, even though it might not be popular. | ❏ | ❏ |

Answers: **1, Yes; 2, No; 3, Yes; 4, Yes.**

When should you *not* express your opinion? Obviously, if you are really not sure of yourself, it's best to reserve comment. Likewise, if the timing is poor or the climate is wrong, silence is preferable. And if the only reason you feel like disagreeing is for the sake of disagreement, by all means withhold your conflicting opinion. Save views that may cause conflict for situations in which you have strong convictions that you can back up with facts.

## C A S E   # 2 :   O O P S !   D I D   I   S A Y   T H A T ?

*In a moment of frustration with a teammate, you have said something you regret. What can you do? Write your answer below, and compare it with the answer on page 87.*

_____

_____

_____

_____

_____

# UNDERSTANDING THE NATURE OF TEAM CONFLICT

How well do you understand the nature of conflict? Test your familiarity by deciding whether the statements below are **TRUE** or **FALSE**.

|  | **TRUE** | **FALSE** |
|---|---|---|
| 1. We can avoid conflict through effective communication and good management. | ❏ | ❏ |
| 2. In a conflict, clearly state your position so that the other person knows where you stand. | ❏ | ❏ |
| 3. Conflicts are always the source of blowups. | ❏ | ❏ |
| 4. Encourage teammates to talk about the <u>real</u> issues causing the conflict. | ❏ | ❏ |
| 5. You should deal with the conflict after teammates have had time to cool off. | ❏ | ❏ |
| 6. If you're the person responsible for resolving the conflict, you must be controlled and have your act together. | ❏ | ❏ |
| 7. Don't vary your style if you're the one responsible for the conflict — it's confusing. | ❏ | ❏ |
| 8. You shouldn't do anything to increase the tension caused by a conflict. | ❏ | ❏ |

Surprise! Every single one of the eight beliefs above is **FALSE**.

## EIGHT WRONG IDEAS ABOUT TEAM CONFLICTS

Conflict can be a positive force in the workplace, but today's fast-paced business world can breed destructive conflict. More demands create more conflicts. Further, the situation seems to be worsening because of the numerous myths that surround conflict resolution.

Here's why these eight "wrong ideas" can prevent your team from building constructive conflict.

• **"We can avoid conflict through effective communication and good management."** Elaine Yarbrough, a conflict-management consultant to major corporations, claims that this is impossible. We must learn to live with and manage conflict, she says.

• **"In a conflict, clearly state your position so that the other person knows where you stand."** Because your position is probably obvious, this often won't help much. What's important is that you actively *try to understand* your adversary's viewpoint.

- **"Conflicts are always the source of blowups."** As Yarbrough indicates, blowups are seldom related to the original conflict. They begin with a minor point that becomes overinflated and causes a misinterpretation of the disputants' true interests.

- **"Encourage teammates to talk about the real issues causing the conflict."** People's best interests are the issues that spark conflict. The problem is that many of us know our positions but not our true best interests.

- **"You should deal with the conflict after teammates have had time to cool off."** This strategy, Yarbrough maintains, is totally wrong. Delaying a resolution can give teammates more time to build up resentment toward one another. Tackle the conflict immediately.

- **"If you're the person responsible for resolving the conflict, you must be controlled and have your act together."** According to the consultant, you won't resolve a conflict unless you are concerned about it and at least partially vulnerable.

- **"Don't vary your style if you're the one responsible for the conflict — it's confusing."** This leads to rigidity. If you're inflexible and don't know when to back off or move in, a mutually beneficial agreement can't be reached.

- **"You shouldn't do anything to increase the tension caused by a conflict."** There are times when you must play for bigger stakes. For example, cite the consequences to your team if you fail to reach accord.

## "COOPERATIVE CONFLICT" IS NO CONTRADICTION

If all eight concepts above are wrong, then what's a team member to do about conflict?

First and foremost, don't avoid it. Learn how to manage conflict and use it to your team's advantage.

"The best possible world is where everyone is attempting to reach the best possible solution together, but where people feel free to challenge one another in the process," says Alfie Kahn, author of *The Case Against Competition* (Houghton Mifflin).

Here's how to create an environment of cooperative conflict:

- **Seek cooperation.** "Even if co-workers are friendly with each other, chances are they have not been in a situation that requires them to depend on — and be accountable for — each other," says Kahn. That feeling must be developed by having everyone aim for the same goal, share the same resources, and receive the same awards.

- **Be sure team members feel safe.** "Everyone should understand that just because their ideas are being challenged does not mean that their authority or competence is being called into question," says Kahn. "No matter how heated a discussion may become, participants should always take care to avoid personal attacks." You're all in this together.

- **Aim for a consensus.** Modify decisions until each team member is satisfied. This encourages a productive discussion more than making a decision by vote. In addition, when all members feel that they have ownership of an idea, the support that idea receives is going to be much more universal.

"Remember that the point of expressing disagreement is not to put others down or promote oneself; it's to reach the best possible decision as a group," says Kahn.

## CASE #3: RESOLVING CONFLICT BETWEEN MEMBERS

*Ben and Ernie are hard workers who care deeply about the success of their team, which manages production for three products in an electronics company. They share responsibility for one stage in the process. Problems have arisen recently, however, because each one has a different way of conducting that particular manufacturing process. Teammates are tired of constantly being corrected as they switch back and forth between methods. Also, some quality concerns have arisen recently. This conflict needs to be resolved, preferably by choosing one of the two methods as the team's preferred manufacturing process. What can be done?*

_____

_____

_____

_____

_____

Compare your answer to the answer on page 87.

## TAMING CONFLICTS

Kenneth Kaye outlines a systematic approach to conflict resolution in *Workplace Wars and How to End Them* (AMACOM). As you review the five sequences involved, reflect on how you can apply them to a conflict brewing on your team.

### Plan A: Look for shared goals, win-win situations

"A conflict becomes merely a problem when the whole group can brainstorm together and act cooperatively to tackle it," Kaye explains.

The techniques used in Plan A begin with *active listening*. Learn to listen well and teach your teammates to do so. You must sort out your goals and encourage everyone to be candid about their attitudes toward everyone's objectives.

Think for a moment about a conflict eating away at your team. What common ground can you find? What goals do you and your teammates share that might serve as an outcome for this conflict? You might make this an exercise during your next meeting, and write answers down on another sheet of paper.

_____

_____

_____

_____

## Plan B: Clarify, sort, value differences

Not everyone is going to share goals, concerns, and perceptions. It's the team leader's task to take sources of conflict and convert them into strengths. Emphasize that the best teamwork comes through diversity.

Look at the list of goals named during your meeting. What similarities emerge? What strengths can you find?

_____

_____

_____

_____

## Plan C: Gain commitment to change

This step calls for tactics to shift team members away from placing blame and toward changing their own behavior. Says Kaye, "The words _change_ and _resist_ are like heads and tails of the same coin. The more change occurs or is proposed, the more resistance will be encountered. Getting people to change may require reassuring them that the needed changes are really very small, under control, and aren't directed by others."

What changes will the resolution to the conflict require? How can you reassure team members that they are small, under control, and are entirely up to them to implement?

_____

_____

_____

_____

_____

## Plan D: Analyze the recurring cycle

If the dispute doesn't disappear, your opportunity is to identify and then use the repetitive patterns in conflicts as the key to resolution.

Analyze these patterns, block them, and bolster the team by substituting constructive patterns that will generate more thoughtful behavior. But, Kaye concedes, real organizational change requires tools that lead to actions more than insights.

What patterns can you see in repetitive conflicts?

_____

_____

_____

_____

_____

How can you use these patterns to help resolve the conflict?

_____

_____

_____

_____

_____

## Plan E: Unilaterally demonstrate change

"Plans B, C, and D may lead you — or one of the other parties — to conclude that the other people in the conflict aren't going to change," Kaye remarks. "This still leaves one approach to try before you give up: unilateral change. Even if only one person changes, everyone else will be able to respond to something different."

How can you change in a way that helps minimize or resolve the conflict?

_____

_____

_____

_____

# ARE YOUR CONFLICTS CONSTRUCTIVE OR DESTRUCTIVE?

Well-handled conflict can bring positive results to your team when constructive conflict lends itself to open communication and negotiation. Do you participate in constructive or destructive conflict? Check **YES** or **NO** in the following assessment and decide.

|  | YES | NO |
|---|---|---|
| 1. I blame those who are at fault. | ❏ | ❏ |
| 2. I search for solutions to conflict. | ❏ | ❏ |
| 3. I allow others to "push my buttons." | ❏ | ❏ |
| 4. I try to gain additional information. | ❏ | ❏ |
| 5. I explain my point of view to others. | ❏ | ❏ |
| 6. I use negotiation whenever I can. | ❏ | ❏ |
| 7. I judge others. | ❏ | ❏ |
| 8. I believe it is possible to have more than one right answer. | ❏ | ❏ |
| 9. If I know I'm right, I don't listen to others; don't try to convince me otherwise. | ❏ | ❏ |
| 10. I get drawn into bickering occasionally. | ❏ | ❏ |

The following are the the correct answers followed by the reason. Note that DC stands for destructive conflict, and CC stands for constructive conflict. **1. NO, DC; 2. YES, CC; 3. NO, DC; 4.YES, CC; 5. YES, CC; 6.YES, CC; 7. NO, DC; 8. YES, CC; 9. NO, DC; 10. NO, DC.** If you answered correctly in nine or 10 instances, you avoid destructive conflict and use constructive conflict to your advantage. If you answered fewer than nine items correctly, you need to modify your destructive responses to conflict.

# 5

# Working with Others Outside Your Team

## INTRODUCTION

In this session you will accomplish the following:

- Assess your team's progress

- Learn ways to welcome a new member to your team

- Boost your service to internal customers

- Enhance your ability to work with other teams

- Measure and increase interteam communication

- Evaluate your team's core disciplines.

# ARE YOU OFF TO A GOOD START?

If you've worked as a team member for six months, it's a good idea to review how well you are adapting to the concept of teamwork. The following assessment can help you determine whether you're off to a good start. Answer each question **YES** or **NO**, then score yourself.

|  | YES | NO |
|---|---|---|
| 1. Do you believe work teams improve communication? | ❏ | ❏ |
| 2. Do you believe work teams increase productivity? | ❏ | ❏ |
| 3. Has communication between you and your co-workers improved? | ❏ | ❏ |
| 4. Do you enjoy the work you do? | ❏ | ❏ |
| 5. Though you may not always agree with your team members, do you respect them overall? | ❏ | ❏ |
| 6. Do you believe your team is making positive contributions to meeting the agenda of your company? | ❏ | ❏ |
| 7. Do you strive for good relations with your fellow team members? | ❏ | ❏ |
| 8. Has your motivation increased? | ❏ | ❏ |
| 9. Has working with others helped broaden your perspective? | ❏ | ❏ |
| 10. Has teamwork helped bring out the best in you? | ❏ | ❏ |

**Total Number of YES Answers:** _____

Eight to 10 **YES** answers show that you have successfully accepted the new approaches you are encountering in teamwork; five to seven, and you are on your way. A lower score indicates you are fighting the concept. Learn more about the value of teamwork in your workplace.

New members who join an existing team face great obstacles. The team already works comfortably together and may seem difficult to penetrate. How can you help a new member become a welcome and productive team member quickly?

- **Start slow.** You don't want to force a newcomer on the group. It takes time for both the group and the new person to be at ease with each other. Even an outgoing person can have a hard time breaking into a close-knit team, and settling in is especially hard for a shy person.

- **Provide frequent assurances.** An outsider is bound to feel alienated and alone. Provide personal assurances through conversations about work-related matters. Help this person gain confidence, which will make him or her more relaxed in the group.

- **Involve him or her in group discussions.** Try this approach: When discussing a problem with several other members of a group, say something like, "Let's see what Sondra thinks of this. She might have some good ideas." You want the others to begin feeling that the outsider is someone who may have a lot to offer.

- **Define your terms.** Let the new person know about any special terms, phrases, or nicknames your team may have coined for its work or one another.

- **"Quote" the newcomer.** Do this discretely. You don't want to appear to value his or her opinion more than you do the opinions of other team members. But on occasion you can pass along ideas and suggestions. This shows not only that you value him or her but that he or she has a valuable contribution to make.

- **Give it time.** Group dynamics change whenever a new person is introduced. It takes time for people to adjust. Don't push it. You don't want someone to feel left out, but a period of adjustment has a natural course to run. In time, he or she will be accepted as a "regular."

# HOW INVITING IS YOUR WELCOME?

How long does it take for new members to fit into your team? While it can be difficult for new members to assimilate information in a short time, it's also true that team members may put up barriers, consciously or unconsciously, to the orientation process. To see how much you help new teammates succeed, take the following assessment, based on a guide by James L. Lundy in *T.E.A.M.S.: Together Each Achieves More Success* (Dartnell).

|  | YES | NO |
|---|---|---|
| 1. Do you clarify the team's goals, resources, and expected performance and results? | ❏ | ❏ |
| 2. Is team building stressed to newcomers? | ❏ | ❏ |
| 3. Are they introduced to everyone with whom they'll be working? | ❏ | ❏ |
| 4. Do you clearly outline team policies, procedures, and standards of ethics? | ❏ | ❏ |
| 5. Is there a tour given of your workplace? | ❏ | ❏ |
| 6. Does a supervisor review such matters as overtime rules, incentives, and benefits? | ❏ | ❏ |
| 7. Are newcomers given copies of team handbooks, procedure manuals, and other basics? | ❏ | ❏ |
| 8. Do you frequently ask new teammates if they have any questions or requests? | ❏ | ❏ |
| 9. If they get off to a good start, do you comment on it and provide encouragement? | ❏ | ❏ |
| 10. Do you invite new members to participate in team social activities, like group lunches? | ❏ | ❏ |

**Total Number of YES Answers:** _____

A perfect score of 10 **YES** answers is essential for creating a welcoming environment for new teammates. Remember how you felt as a team novice and how much a friendly face and good source of information helped.

QUICK TIP

## GOOD START

Join a new team member on the first break of your team meeting. That action sends a clear signal that you are interested and supportive.

## CASE #1: THE UNRESPONSIVE TEAMMATE

*Team dynamics have changed dramatically since Sara joined your group two months ago. She arrives late to meetings, sits in back, and seldom contributes to the group discussion. Team members are beginning to ignore her and are increasingly resentful. Productivity and morale have declined.*

What can you do to help Sara become a productive part of the existing team?

_____

_____

_____

_____

_____

_____

Compare your answer with the solution on page 88.

## WHEN NEW TEAM MEMBERS RESIST

Sometimes when new members join your team, they resist a procedure because it's different from the way they *used* to solve problems on their previous team. Their resistance conveys a "That won't work!" attitude that can hinder your team's ability to work successfully.

When new members think your team's way will not work, they have logical reasons. This usually occurs as a problem when employees are new to the job or when you introduce a new approach or technique to someone who has performed that task for a long time.

Try this approach when a new teammate resists:

1. If a teammate really believes that a technique or process is unworkable, let her sound off before starting the next project.

2. Ask your team leader to explain why your way will work. Merely telling them isn't good enough; you have to sell them.

3. As a team, furnish the resistant team member with proof that the method will succeed. Nobody can argue with a winning record.

4. If she is still resistant, remind her that you appreciate her point of view, but she must keep in mind that teams function through majority rule.

## ASSESSMENT
## CARING FOR INTERNAL CUSTOMERS

How well do you and your team serve your internal customers? Take this assessment and find out.

|  | YES | NO |
|---|---|---|
| 1. Do you know who your customers are? | ❏ | ❏ |
| 2. Have you asked them what they want from you — what would make their work easier? | ❏ | ❏ |
| 3. Have you talked with the people who supply you — and told them how they can make your work easier? | ❏ | ❏ |
| 4. Do you make an effort to build a rapport with your internal customers by offering to do small favors when they need help? | | |
| 5. Do you avoid arguing with your co-workers — preferring to settle disputes in a friendly fashion? | ❏ | ❏ |
| 6. Do you try to remain cheerful, even if the person you are working with has a poor disposition? | ❏ | ❏ |
| 7. Do you try to be flexible in a crisis? | ❏ | ❏ |
| 8. Do you always look for ways to improve the quality of the work you provide your internal customers? | ❏ | ❏ |

You should have answered **YES** to all of the above questions. Satisfying internal customers requires a flexible and positive approach to work as well as the willingness to help out when necessary. Good social skills help you get things done more easily and are always a career asset.

In many organizations different departments and their employees are literally *each other's customers*. Only when departments can handle the needs of others *internally* can the organization satisfy the external customer. That is why everyday internal customer service can boost profits and maximize your team's results.

By understanding your particular organization, its people, and all of its services, you will know whom to contact if a customer, business associate, or you individually need something that is handled by another department.

Complete the following worksheet to gain a new perspective on the "big picture" and how your team fits. It will help you identify ways to help co-workers and improve your team's ability to service its internal customers.

| Department | Product | Contact |
|---|---|---|
| *(list all company departments)* | *(what departments are responsible for)* | *(who you can call for help)* |

_____

_____

_____

_____

_____

_____

_____

_____

_____

_____

# HOW TO IMPROVE YOUR
# INTERNAL CUSTOMER SERVICE

- **Return phone calls.** When a co-worker calls, get back to him or her quickly. Another employee may need your expertise to serve a client. Also, you'll encourage co-workers to return your calls quickly if that's the treatment they get from you.

- **Share information with others.** If you find a handy tip for performing a task, let others know about it. Share information about new products and services.

- **Help out.** Is that phone at the next desk ringing? Answer it. Does a co-worker need files that you can locate? Retrieve them. Is a colleague trying to serve three customers simultaneously while two more wait? Help out.

- **Communicate.** Too often interdepartmental communication is limited to managers. These people don't do a lot of the hands-on work, so they might not be able to offer the most detailed information. Seek opportunities to get acquainted with co-workers from other departments.

## ASSESSMENT
# SHARE INFORMATION WITH INSIDE CUSTOMERS

No one would dispute the importance of good communication with the customers your company does business with. But what about the importance of communicating with your co-workers — those "customers" you and your team serve within your organization? Information sharing can be a powerful tool to aid colleagues, helping them to do their jobs more easily with fewer errors in less time. It can also nurture a team approach to achieving a shared goal: satisfying the outside customer.

How often do you use the following internal communications methods?

**1. Electronic mail.** How often do you send messages to your network about what you learned by talking to an important customer or how you solved a problem?

| Never | | Rarely | | Sometimes | | | Often | | Always |
|---|---|---|---|---|---|---|---|---|---|
| 1 | 2 | 3 | 4 | 5 | 6 | 7 | 8 | 9 | 10 |

**2. Comment and suggestion forms.** One team that manages a warehouse, plant floor, shipping, and customer service uses special forms to share information about customers, parts needed, problems encountered, and shipping arrangements. They have found that "group involvement" through shared information leads to increased quality, productivity, and service. How often do you take advantage of this kind of internal "suggestion box" to share ideas about ways to do your job better?

| Never | | Rarely | | Sometimes | | | Often | | Always |
|---|---|---|---|---|---|---|---|---|---|
| 1 | 2 | 3 | 4 | 5 | 6 | 7 | 8 | 9 | 10 |

**3. Articles of interest.** How often do you route articles you think co-workers might like to read? Doing so can help everyone benefit from your research.

| Never | | Rarely | | Sometimes | | Often | | Always | |
|---|---|---|---|---|---|---|---|---|---|
| 1 | 2 | 3 | 4 | 5 | 6 | 7 | 8 | 9 | 10 |

**4. Staff meetings.** How often do you use a staff meeting to share information important to your internal customers?

| Never | | Rarely | | Sometimes | | Often | | Always | |
|---|---|---|---|---|---|---|---|---|---|
| 1 | 2 | 3 | 4 | 5 | 6 | 7 | 8 | 9 | 10 |

**5. Department bulletin board.** If company policy allows it, try posting suggestions on how to do jobs more effectively. It's a simple, cost-effective way to distribute information — especially if employees are in the habit of checking the board. How often do you practice the "posting" habit?

| Never | | Rarely | | Sometimes | | Often | | Always | |
|---|---|---|---|---|---|---|---|---|---|
| 1 | 2 | 3 | 4 | 5 | 6 | 7 | 8 | 9 | 10 |

**6. Sharing personal experiences.** Sharing what you've learned during an interaction with a supplier may help an internal customer do his or her job better. By sharing, you not only let others profit from what you have learned but they might share information too. How often do you share personal experiences to let others learn from your victories and mistakes?

| Never | | Rarcly | | Sometimes | | Often | | Always | |
|---|---|---|---|---|---|---|---|---|---|
| 1 | 2 | 3 | 4 | 5 | 6 | 7 | 8 | 9 | 10 |

TOTAL _____

If you scored between 45 and 60 points, you're already passing along important information to your internal customers. If you scored fewer than 45 points, it's time to consider new ways to connect with your internal customers — and to make that kind of sharing a habit.

# WORKING WITH OTHER TEAMS

Do the various teams in your organization know what the others do? To bring everyone up-to-date (and boost efficiency), conduct in-house seminars at which the teams explain their goals and activities to one another.

Your team will become more effective when members learn about the other jobs and work teams within your company. Bring your team together with employees from other departments so they can become acquainted and discuss their jobs. When employees discover the extent to which their work affects other departments, they are likely to become more responsible and quality-conscious.

As you begin to focus on ways your team can support other departments, you will be surprised by how many ideas you generate. And when you start strengthening your relationships with other groups, you will be amazed by how much support comes back to your team.

List the teams you work with most closely, and their functions.

_____

_____

_____

_____

How can your team better support these teams in their work?

_____

_____

_____

_____

What benefits will your team derive from stronger relationships with these teams?

_____

_____

_____

_____

# PAIR UP FOR SUCCESS

*Aldina Fuentes was frustrated. Each month, as production coordinator for a financial printer headquartered in suburban Chicago, she was responsible for tracking scores of pamphlets and brochures. Lately, the accounting department kept changing its paperwork procedures weekly.*

*As a result, Fuentes often had to prepare a new report form after being told that the one she had used the previous week was no longer acceptable. "Virtually nothing at work was routine anymore," she fretted.*

*Rather than grumble about the accounting department, Fuentes asked her boss if she and her co-workers could take advantage of a new company teamwork tool called pairing. In this organization, a pairing project is a way to bring together workers or departments so they can come up with mutual solutions for any difficulties between them.*

*Fuentes related her frustration with the constant change in procedures. The accounting staff listened, then gave their reasons for the changes. As it turned out, the accounting department was shifting to a computerized financial tracking system and was testing various software programs. The result was confusion.*

*The one-hour pairing meeting ended with an increased understanding on both sides. Accounting agreed to announce any changes as early as possible. Production agreed to be more tolerant of the changes. They understood that the situation would be short-term and benefit the company's bottom line.*

In short, pairing is a low-risk, low-cost way to enhance teamwork and efficiency within an organization. It doesn't require special equipment or a big budget. And it generally produces the kind of communication needed for any company to perform at its best. Here are pairing project basics:

- **A facilitator.** This is usually another staff member, but one who has no connection with either party and no vested interest in the issue. The facilitator's job is to keep the discussion moving in a positive direction.

- **Neutral territory.** A conference room, small auditorium, or even small office can be suitable, as long as it provides a degree of privacy.

- **Positive attitudes.** Healthy skepticism is helpful, but participants should not enter into a pairing session predisposed to failure or personal victory. Pairings exist to inform and explain as well as to search for solutions. Most times, misunderstandings or problems are not any single person's "fault." More often, problems are caused by flawed procedures or systems.

- **Follow-ups, as needed.** In Fuentes' case, she invited accountants to take a tour of her work area. During that friendly, informal visit, she was able to give them a better idea of her situation.

A pairing need not be so formalized or group-focused as the one just described. Are you experiencing misunderstanding with a person in another department crucial to what your area does? Maybe a short pairing session with a neutral third party would help. You might be surprised how this information-sharing method can help you build more productive work relationships.

How can you apply pairing to a problem facing your team?

_____

_____

_____

_____

_____

# HOW'S YOUR INTERTEAM COMMUNICATION?

How well do you communicate with other teams? Take this assessment to find out. Answer each question **YES** or **NO**, then check your score.

| | YES | NO |
|---|---|---|
| 1. If teammates seem resistant to communicating outside the team, do you point out potential benefits? | ❑ | ❑ |
| 2. Do you participate freely in meetings? | ❑ | ❑ |
| 3. Are you open-minded about work issues? | ❑ | ❑ |
| 4. Do you talk to members of other teams about their work so you know how they fit in to the big picture? | ❑ | ❑ |
| 5. Are you informed about all levels of your company? | ❑ | ❑ |
| 6. Do you think collaboration is more important than competitiveness among teams? | ❑ | ❑ |
| 7. When a co-worker has a great idea, do you endorse it without feeling inferior? | ❑ | ❑ |
| 8. Do you realize that the quality of your communication affects the company as a whole? | ❑ | ❑ |
| 9. Is expressing your ideas part of your job? | ❑ | ❑ |
| 10. Are you comfortable with the positions you take, even if someone disagrees with you? | ❑ | ❑ |

**Total Number of YES Answers:** _____

A score of eight or more **YES** responses suggests that you participate effectively in your organization. A lower score, however, indicates that you're probably not the person to whom managers and teammates turn when interteam communication is needed to solve a problem.

# STAYING IN TOUCH WHEN YOUR TEAM WORKS DIFFERENT SHIFTS

In team-oriented manufacturing organizations, shift transfers are dealt with in the same way they are in more traditional organizations — through effective communication between teams in both shifts.

Schreiber Foods in Tempe, Arizona, has "communicators" on each team who regularly meet with people on the next shift during transfer time. Members of both teams also occasionally hold formal meetings.

At Becton, Dickinson and Company in Durham, North Carolina, teams actually cross shift boundaries. Through careful coordination and production scheduling, workers from all three shifts manufacture the same product.

Coordination and communication are critical. One team member who performs a process out of sequence for his own convenience may create chaos for everyone else.

How can shift-transfer communication be improved for your team?

_____

_____

_____

_____

The modern business often has a number of offices spread out across a country or even across continents. When you work with people who are removed from your immediate area, it's easy to forget that you all work for the same organization and share the same goals.

But this long-distance operation doesn't dismiss the need for teamwork. In fact, it makes it even more important.

To achieve peak performance, teammates on all levels and at all locations must cooperate. Your support of co-workers who are in the field, at another office, or in another department is key to your ultimate success. Try using these methods to strengthen the lines of communication with your "distant" teammates.

**1. Treat distant teammates like customers.** Customers are responsible for company profits. Co-workers are, too. You go out of your way to serve customers. Teammates deserve that same kind of service.

**2. Make small talk.** Whenever possible, try to talk with your faraway co-workers. If used effectively, the telephone can build bridges. Get to know those co-workers to establish a friendly climate. When people feel positively toward each other, cooperation prospers.

**3. Make clear communication a priority.** Listen carefully. Be *sure* you understand what co-workers need and are asking from you. By providing what your inside customers need, you are indirectly serving your outside customers as well.

**4. Boost the information flow.** Notify a co-worker of delays or complications as soon as possible. For example, if a long-distance co-worker requests a report for tomorrow that you know will take two days to prepare, explain the situation.

**5. Be candid.** Let a co-worker know if he or she has unreasonable expectations. Remember, the long-distance teammate may not be aware that a task cannot be accomplished in the time frame he or she desires. Be candid about what you can do and when. You'll show your co-worker you genuinely do want to work together.

*Salesman Sam's territory is in the Midwest, and he rarely visits or even contacts his Florida home office. Suddenly, he requires updates on product availability and shipping schedules for potential customers.*

*The only way Sam can get up-to-the-minute data is via the sales support team in the Florida office. He phones frequently — many calls come in at 4:45 P.M. when Florida personnel leave for the day. The sales support team doesn't say anything, but they discuss his calls among themselves.*

*They decide not to answer the phone after 4:30 p.m. and since they think of Sam as a nuisance, they don't always bother to obtain the latest figures and data. Thus, Sam works at a disadvantage — and so does his company. A competitor is able to provide potential customers with quick answers to questions, while Sam must wait to obtain crucial data that may not come in for days.*

As a result, Sam's sales performance is slipping and the Midwest region's market share is declining. How can this team improve its support for Sam and correct the situation that has led to such bad feelings?

_____

_____

_____

_____

_____

_____

Compare your answer to the solution on page 88.

# HOW ARE YOUR CORE DISCIPLINES?

Putting a team structure in place isn't enough to guarantee its success. What ensures a team's success is its ability to pay attention to the details of teamwork, defined in the 13 core disciplines listed here. Assess your team's performance on each of these disciplines, using a scale of **1 = Never, 3 = Sometimes,** and **5 = Always.**

**1. Customer focus.** My team knows who its customers are and considers how changes may affect them.

| 1 | 2 | 3 | 4 | 5 |
|---|---|---|---|---|
| Never | | Sometimes | | Always |

**2. Purpose.** My team is highly focused and has a clear mission statement.

| 1 | 2 | 3 | 4 | 5 |
|---|---|---|---|---|
| Never | | Sometimes | | Always |

**3. Principles.** We have developed guiding principles to help in decision making.

| 1 | 2 | 3 | 4 | 5 |
|---|---|---|---|---|
| Never | | Sometimes | | Always |

**4. Boundaries.** Each team member understands the constraints under which the team must operate.

| 1 | 2 | 3 | 4 | 5 |
|---|---|---|---|---|
| Never | | Sometimes | | Always |

**5. Communication.** My team has clearly defined acceptable and unacceptable team-interaction behaviors.

| 1 | 2 | 3 | 4 | 5 |
|---|---|---|---|---|
| Never | | Sometimes | | Always |

**6. Roles.** We regularly discuss our roles and changes needed in those roles to accomplish team tasks.

| 1 | 2 | 3 | 4 | 5 |
|---|---|---|---|---|
| Never | | Sometimes | | Always |

**7. Accountability.** In my team there is strong individual and team accountability.

| 1 | 2 | 3 | 4 | 5 |
|---|---|---|---|---|
| Never | | Sometimes | | Always |

**8. Decision making.** Team members feel empowered to take immediate action to satisfy customer needs.

| 1 | 2 | 3 | 4 | 5 |
|---|---|---|---|---|
| Never | | Sometimes | | Always |

**9. Problem solving.** My team has a broad knowledge of problem-solving tools and methods.

| 1 | 2 | 3 | 4 | 5 |
|---|---|---|---|---|
| Never | | Sometimes | | Always |

**10. Feedback.** My team members are skilled at giving and receiving feedback.

| 1 | 2 | 3 | 4 | 5 |
|---|---|---|---|---|
| Never | | Sometimes | | Always |

**11. Work redesign.** We are highly focused on improving work methods and processes.

| 1 | 2 | 3 | 4 | 5 |
|---|---|---|---|---|
| Never | | Sometimes | | Always |

**12. Continual learning.** Our team understands the concept of continuous learning.

| 1 | 2 | 3 | 4 | 5 |
|---|---|---|---|---|
| Never | | Sometimes | | Always |

**13. Continual improvement.** We regularly take time to assess our strengths and weaknesses and develop plans for improvement.

| 1 | 2 | 3 | 4 | 5 |
|---|---|---|---|---|
| Never | | Sometimes | | Always |

How are your core disciplines? If your team scored a three or lower on any of these disciplines, consider remedial training in that area.

# Conclusion:
# Your Action Plan

As you have worked through the exercises in this book, you have probably identified areas in which you need to strengthen your teamwork skills. You may also have identified areas in which your team needs to improve in order to be productive.

Now's your chance to summarize those strengths, pinpoint any weaknesses, and commit to improving your problem-solving skills.

Circle the areas in which your strengths are most solid.

- **Clarifying team mission and goals**

- **Defining team roles and responsibilities**

- **Contributing to a healthy team climate**

- **Building team trust**

- **Giving and receiving feedback**

- **Resolving team conflict**

- **Running productive team meetings**

- **Working with other teams**

- **Serving your internal customers**

Now, list your plans to enhance the skills that you did not circle. What can you do to improve in each area? What can your team do? Be sure to identify specific steps as well as dates by which you plan to implement them.

### Clarifying team mission and goals

What you can do:

_____

_____

_____

What your team can do:

_____

_____

_____

### Defining team roles and responsibilities

What you can do:

_____

_____

_____

What your team can do:

_____

_____

_____

### Contributing to a healthy team climate

What you can do:

_____

_____

_____

What your team can do:

_____

_____

_____

**Building team trust**

What you can do:

_____

_____

_____

What your team can do:

_____

_____

_____

**Giving and receiving feedback**

What you can do:

_____

_____

_____

What your team can do:

_____

_____

_____

**Resolving team conflict**

What you can do:

_____

_____

_____

What your team can do:

_____

_____

_____

## Running productive team meetings

What you can do:

_____

_____

_____

What your team can do:

_____

_____

_____

## Working with other teams

What you can do:

_____

_____

_____

What your team can do:

_____

_____

_____

## Serving your internal customers

What you can do:

_____

_____

_____

What your team can do:

_____

_____

_____

Best wishes for a successful team future!

# A P P E N D I X :   A N S W E R S

## Answer to Session 4 Case #1: "Nothing's Wrong, Right?"

Simply take your co-worker literally about "nothing being wrong," advises management consultant and author Marilyn Moats Kennedy. She suggests saying to your fellow team member, "I'm really glad nothing is wrong, because if there were I'd like to try to do something about it. How about lunch?"

Kennedy says this puts your associate on the spot. If there's nothing wrong, as claimed, having lunch with you is the only polite thing to do. Begin increasing contact — join in at breaks and chat cheerfully before your work team meets.

Why this approach?

Kennedy says this forces your fellow team member to either warm up to you or to break down and admit that something is wrong. If he has made comments to other people, you owe it to yourself to improve the relationship or at least determine the problem. This assertive approach usually resolves it one way or the other.

## Answer to Session 4 Case #2: "Oops! Did I Say That?"

Take these steps to correct the situation.

• Apologize immediately. If you wait, bad feelings can mushroom.

• Don't fan the flames. If an apology isn't enough, don't drag it on by continuously apologizing or bringing up the subject. Instead, make every effort to conduct yourself in such a way as to show that you didn't mean any harm.

• Actions speak louder than words. Give it time.

• Forgive yourself. You can't turn back the clock and change what you've said. But you can learn from the experience. Teach yourself to take a breath before you speak when you're discussing a heated issue. And find a lesson in the experience: Learn to be more forgiving of others who commit the same error with you.

## Answer to Session 4 Case #3: "Resolving Conflict Between Members"

"When two team members don't get along, it may be time to call on your best skills as a negotiator," says Glen Varney, author of *Building Productive Teams: An Action Guide and Resource Book* (Jossey-Bass).

He notes, however, that there are three conditions that must be met if negotiation is going to succeed:

1. **Both teammates must stand to gain from a negotiated solution.**

2. **Each will attain some power.**

3. **The two are interdependent. In other words, each needs the other to complete work.**

Varney suggests that the team leader bring the disputants together and ask the individuals these questions:

- "As you see it, what's the problem?"

- "What does Ben (or Ernie) do that contributes to the problem?"

- "What do you want or need from him?"

- "What do you do that adds to the problem?"

- "Can you suggest the first step to resolve this situation?"

Ben and Ernie then take turns answering questions. They can let off steam, but each must admit partial responsibility.

The third party should keep them in a problem-solving mood. Soon, they're bound to agree on an action plan. To avoid misunderstandings, get it in writing.

## Answer to Session 5 Case #1: "The Unresponsive Teammate"

Because Sara is obviously shy, both the group leader and the team members need to go the extra mile to include Sara. Perhaps the team leader could watch Sara closely and notice when she seems about to say something. Then the leader can intervene and ask her opinion. There's a good chance that, if asked, she will provide intelligent and useful suggestions.

Other team members should follow the leader's cue and watch for opportunities to include Sara. In time, she will begin asserting herself without coaxing.

## Answer to Session 5 Case #2: "Requesting Information"

As you can see, lack of cooperation works against potential sales and profits. All callers to the Florida office are entitled to be welcomed up until closing time. Conversely, Salesman Sam shouldn't expect lengthy reports when co-workers are leaving for the day.

Instead of building hostility toward Sam, the workers in the home office could remind him of the difference in time zones. They could explain that everyone is preparing for the next day at 4:30 P.M. and that they could serve him better if he called earlier. Sam may not realize that his expectations are unreasonable. If you are candid with him, chances are good that he will begin to comply — and the long-distance working relationship will be healed.